The Gendered Landscape

A discussion on gender, status and power in the Norwegian Viking Age landscape

Marianne Moen

BAR International Series 2207
2011

Published in 2016 by
BAR Publishing, Oxford

BAR International Series 2207

The Gendered Landscape

ISBN 978 1 4073 0765 7

© M Moen and the Publisher 2011

The author's moral rights under the 1988 UK Copyright,
Designs and Patents Act are hereby expressly asserted.

All rights reserved. No part of this work may be copied, reproduced, stored,
sold, distributed, scanned, saved in any form of digital format or transmitted
in any form digitally, without the written permission of the Publisher.

BAR Publishing is the trading name of British Archaeological Reports (Oxford) Ltd.
British Archaeological Reports was first incorporated in 1974 to publish the BAR
Series, International and British. In 1992 Hadrian Books Ltd became part of the BAR
group. This volume was originally published by Archaeopress in conjunction with
British Archaeological Reports (Oxford) Ltd / Hadrian Books Ltd, the Series principal
publisher, in 2011. This present volume is published by BAR Publishing, 2016.

Printed in England

BAR titles are available from:

              BAR Publishing
              122 Banbury Rd, Oxford, OX2 7BP, UK
EMAIL   info@barpublishing.com
PHONE +44 (0)1865 310431
  FAX   +44 (0)1865 316916
              www.barpublishing.com

CHAPTER 1. INTRODUCTION 2

1.1 Introductory statement – aims and objectives 3
1.2 Mortuary evidence 3
1.3 Gender and mortuary evidence – a past populated by men? 5
1.4 Gender expressed in the landscape 8
1.5 An outline of what is to follow 9

CHAPTER 2. PREVIOUS RESEARCH 10

2.1 The history of Viking studies in Norway 10
2.2 Gender studies 11
2.3 Landscape – finally looking past things 13
2.4 Conclusion 13

CHAPTER 3. THE VIKING AGE – A WIDER CONTEXT   15

3.1 'Religion', belief systems and the ritual landscape 15
3.2 Gender identities and roles 17
3.3 The landscape of power – can we read social status from landscape? 18
3.4 Conclusion 19

CHAPTER 4. THE OSEBERG BURIAL 20

4.1. The Oseberg find 20
4.2. Description of the find 20
4.3 The barrow's positioning in the landscape 21
4.3 The Oseberg women 26
4.4 Conclusion 28

CHAPTER 5. THE CEMETERIES AT KAUPANG 29

5.1 The Kaupang case 29
5.2 The Kaupang Landscape 29
5.3 Nordre Kaupang and Hagejordet 32
5.4 Lamøya 34
5.5 Bikjholberget 35
5.6 Conclusion 37

CHAPTER 6. DISCUSSION 38

6.1 Summary of findings 38
6.2 Women on the margins: of Viking Age social order or archaeological interpretation? 38
6.3 Power and influence, the different faces of status 39
6.4 Female power: witches, shield maidens and matrons? 40
6.5 Kaupang and Oseberg – exceptional or representative of a wider trend? 42
6.6 Conclusion 44

CHAPTER 7. CONCLUSION 46

Table 48

Bibliography 74

List of illustrations:

Figure 1. Map of Vestfold with important sites from the Iron Age — 4
Figure 2. Map showing Raet — 23
Figure 3. The Oseberg mound seen from a distance — 24
Figure 4. View from the Oseberg mound — 25
Figure 5. View from the Gokstad mound — 26
Figure 6 and 7. The two staffs found in the Oseberg ship — 28
Figure 8. Reconstruction of the Kaupang area as it would have appeared in the Viking Age — 31
Figure 9. Map of the Kaupang cemeteries — 32
Figure 10. Map of the graves of Nordre Kaupang in relation to the probable route of the road — 33
Figure 11. Male to female ratio of sexed graves at Nordre Kaupang — 34
Figure 12. Male to female ratio of gendered graves at Lamøya — 35
Figure 13. Male to female ratio at Bikjholberget — 37
Figure 14. Possible Volve staff — 41

Chapter 1. Introduction

This chapter will outline the aims and objectives for this study. In order to give a theoretical background for the evidence which will be presented in following chapters, I will start with a discussion of the main categories of evidence used: mortuary evidence, gendered evidence and the landscape. An outline of the structure and contents of the paper will also be included.

1.1 Introductory statement – aims and objectives

This study is the result of a long standing interest in the expression of social identities of the past, perhaps more specifically, social identities as translated through gender, and their resulting cultural expressions and material remains.

The overarching subject I wish to explore is the gender structures prevalent in the Late Iron Age in the county of Vestfold, Norway (for a geographical overview of the aerea, please see Figure 1). The Scandinavian Late Iron Age, popularly known as the Viking Age, is often represented as deeply and inherently male, with male aggressiveness as the ideal presented to the public, leaving little room for alternative gender roles in the popular imagination (Jesch 1994:1). Gender is one of the basic structuring principles of most societies (Skogstrand 2002:121), and as a social category it must be understood in order to grasp the cultural complexity of a society. I will attempt to show that the gender roles of the Viking Age are perhaps often interpreted and represented too simplistically, and that popular stereotypes fail to take into account the complex multitude of categories, variations and negotiations which one ought to expect from the interpretation of gender. My basic proposition is that if the gender roles of the Viking Age were more complex than what is often believed, this may be reflected in the mortuary landscape and in the choice of location for burials: if there was sharp gender segregation in terms of social importance, this ought arguably to be reflected in burial customs. If it is not, this may lead towards a re-examination of the traditional gender roles assigned to the Late Iron Age.

In order to approach this subject, I will look at the relative positioning of female graves in the mortuary landscape of the Viking Age, and I have chosen to focus on two different sites in the county now known as Vestfold: Oseberg and Kaupang. The choice of these two sites in particular was dominated by concerns including that they are both well documented, and have received a lot of attention in archaeological research. These considerations make the sites approachable for an author lacking the option of carrying out independent field research, and also amenable for a study which relies on earlier research in order to re-examine established views of the past, as I aim to do here. The sites represent different burial traditions, Oseberg being of a monumental nature in rural surroundings, whilst Kaupang represents a wider selection of graves connected to a busy trading port. However, the assumption that they are comparable as representing some of the same ideology behind the death rituals is defensible. Further, they represent different tiers of social strata, and thus together form a stronger case study than a single-site focus would yield. It is my belief that if the mortuary landscape is to tell us anything of the gender ideologies of the past, this must be observable at more than one site.

In order to give a background to my discussion, I will use the remainder of this chapter to set out my views on the interpretation of gender, especially in mortuary evidence in the Late Iron Age context of landscape.

1.2 Mortuary evidence

The mortuary record is arguably one of the most useful sources available to the archaeologist, perhaps because it is made up of evidence which has been deposited intentionally rather than accidentally and thus differs from some other types of finds. It also represents the physical traces of ritual and social actions, and can thus be seen as an imprint of past beliefs and ways of structuring the world. As Grete Lillehammer has suggested, understanding burial evidence is about structuring the physical remnants of a 'funeral' into patters which can be read and understood (Lillehammer 1996a:13). If the grave is understood as a symbol, or as the remains of a social act which was loaded with symbolism (the burial rites), it can be assumed that this symbol can provide information about how the society in question communicated, at least in terms of their religious beliefs (Lillehammer 1996a:95). If the grave is understood as the expression of rituals and therey beliefs, it can be used to understand past social actions and practices (Tsigoridas 1998:1). It is the action behind the burial (Lia 2002:293), and the meaning embedded in it, that we want to understand. If, as Hodder as suggested 'meaning is not just meaning. It is always of someone and for someone' (Hodder 2007:31) we should be looking at how meaning was structured and understood in the past.

Paradoxically, burial evidence is amongst the most studied categories of archaeological evidence, yet also amongst the least understood (Frabregd in Stylegar 1997:69). In Scandinavia at least, the study of mortuary evidence has given us a number of the basic building blocks of archaeology, such as typologies and chronologies (Stylegar 1997:69), and it is hard to imagine what archaeological study of the Viking Age would be like without this evidence readily to hand. And yet, the deeper understanding of the inherent symbolism and beliefs behind the ritual actions is difficult to obtain.

The Gendered Landscape

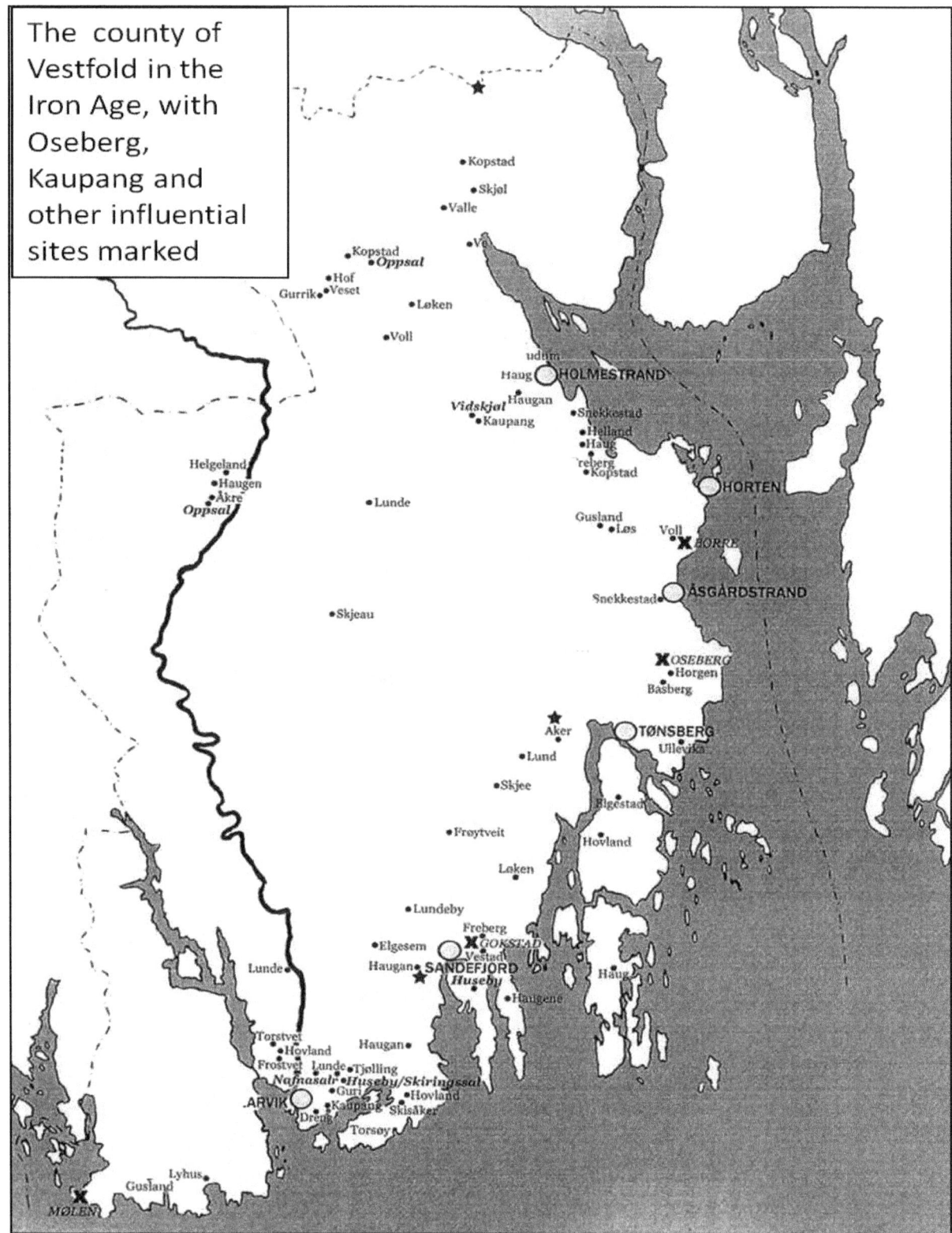

Fig. 1. Map of Vestfold with important sites from the Iron Age marked in (reproduced from Stylegar and Skre 2004:72).

It is a truism to state that death is a universal fact, whilst burial rites are culturally loaded and consequently culturally dependent actions (Lillehammer 1996a:97; Stylegar 1997:80). Nevertheless it is a truism which is crucial to the interpretation of the mortuary record, if we are to go on the assumption that death rituals reflect social structures. My belief is that the mortuary record to some degree reflects a society's beliefs in death, life and the afterlife. In order to understand the resulting expression of past death beliefs, the evidence available needs to be examined in terms of categories which include:

- Inner and outer shape of the burial

Chapter 1: Introduction

- Where possible, the sex, age and physical attributes of the deceased, i.e. the individual buried (Lillehammer 1996a:97)

- Accompanying grave goods

- Location of the grave, seen in terms of its relative positioning in relation to other graves, habitation areas and other features in the landscape, both natural and man-made.

By examining these categories, I believe we can start to build an understanding of the underlying reasons for the various rituals we see expressed in the archaeological evidence. A burial will often be created out of consideration for the living, or respect for the dead, but also for the benefit of the deceased and their passage to the afterlife (Lillehammer 1996a:97). The burial may be aimed at preparing the dead for the afterlife, and if this is the case, we can perhaps expect some degree of exaggeration or glorification of the deceased, in order to ensure the individual made a grand entrance to this new phase of their existence (Kristoffersen and Oestigaard 2008:136).

Of course it must be remembered that what is seen may be a reflection of those who carried out the burial, rather than the actual deceased (Lillehammer 1996a:100), or that it may be a glorified and exaggerated image of ritual belief. It is possible that status expressed in burials may not directly correlate to the individual buried, and that burials may reflect wider concerns such as family and social ties (Lillehammer 1996b:63). These concerns have often been presented as an argument against making too many inferences on rank and status on the basis of mortuary evidence (Stalsberg 2001:74). However, I believe it reasonable to assume that the material remains are often a reflection of rituals carried out for the living, but in honour of the dead, which would make it likely we are faced with evidence representative of the identity of the dead, and the rituals deemed appropriate on the part of the living to accord with that person's social standing. In the case of Vestfold, this is based on the variety of burial rites represented, which indicates that different concerns governed the inner and outer markings, as well as the grave goods. This may be seen to point towards a burial treatment according to concerns such as status, social standing and social identity.

1.3 Gender and mortuary evidence – a past populated by men?

As established above then, the mortuary record is potentially a rich source of information about past rituals, beliefs, cultural and social structures. Consequently, it is a source of information about past gender structures, and as has already been mentioned, gender can be seen as one of the most fundamental structuring principles for social organisation (Skogstrand 2006:109). A brief introduction to the genesis of gender archaeology will follow in Chapter 2, and therefore will not be touched on here. Suffice to say that gender as a structuring category is a basic building stone without which I do not believe that the past can be studied in a useful or meaningful way. An understanding of the gender roles, identities and social standing will be essential in forming a meaningful idea of the workings of any society.

At this stage it will be useful to take a brief look at the sex versus gender debate, in order to clarify the ideas presented and language used in this study. Throughout the early stages of gender archaeology, sex was largely accepted as a biological fact, a relatively stable and fixed category, whereas gender was seen as culturally dependent, and consequently fluid and changeable (Arnold 2002:240). In the words of Simone de Beavoir 'One is not born a woman, but rather one becomes a woman' (de Beavoir in Gilchrist 1999:9). The overarching idea is that gender goes beyond physical attributes, and can be recognised as a set of roles, rules and behaviours (Kearney 2008:247). The debate of nature versus nurture is important and although it will not be fully explored here, it is worth touching on some aspects. The categories of biological sex and cultural gender are of relevance here, in particular how these are interpreted socially. In recent decades, the sex/gender division has become contested, as a result of theorists such as Judith Butler, who through her Queer theory has questioned the assumption that sex can be called a universal biological fact (Fallander 2006:27; Haugen 2009:12). This type of questioning is useful in that it points out to us the caution required to avoid the pitfalls of presentism and ethnocentrism: it cannot be assumed that all societies and cultures share our deep-set belief in biology as a given truth (Gilchrist 1999:9). However, many gender archaeologists feel it is hard to follow Queer theory and study gender usefully at the same time (Arnold 2002:240), and for purposes of clarification, I accept gender as codified and institutionalised socially and culturally (Hylland Eriksen 1995:125), and sex as a category tied to the physical body, which in turn is recognised as a structuring category in most known societies (Skogstrand 2002:109). The relevant variable is the interpretation of what the subsequent gender categories entail, and the values attached to the various gender options. Gender as a message communicated through garment, ornament, and social role, has considerable room for variations that we ought not underestimate. What can be stated with some certainty however, is that the body is not a given (Joyce 2007:84), and that this contributes to the fluidity of gender as a category. A persons gender identity will be modified from a variety of factors, such as age and status (Gilchrist 2007:142), and so there is no 'one size fits all' in terms of gender models. There is no such thing as a universal male or female experience (Fuglestvedt 2006:56), and consequently we ought to expect a spectrum of different gender expressions in any one society.

Another issue of interest here, is the disproportional amount of importance traditionally awarded the 'male' sphere, very often talked of as the 'public', and how this makes 'women's work' in the household and 'private' sphere secondary and of less importance (Fuglestvedt 2006:49). According to western tradition, male attributes include being more aggressive and competitive, whilst women are more nurturing, weaker and dependent on the strength of men (Conkey and Spector 1998:18; Doucette 2001:170; Gilchrist 1999:10). This value division is a result of western ideals developed in the last few centuries, and anthropology as well as history has taught us that they cannot be assumed to be universal, as is observable in the different expressions of gender ideology documented from different cultures (see for example Gilchrist 1999:14). There is always a danger of subscribing to a 'gender mythology' in the study of the past, which draws on stereotypes rather than posing open questions and asking questions (Gilchrist 2007:142). It has in fact often been pointed out that contemporary western society is relatively poor in terms of gender categories (Arnold 2002:240), and this may contribute to a narrow understanding of the past. The question must be asked if the division of public and private the way it is seen in modern western society is applicable to social structures in the Late Iron Age, and 'the politically constituted mature of knowledge production and its historical embededness' (di Ronaldo in Arwill-Nordbladh 1998:52) must be highlighted. These distinctions are important to set out, but sadly not always accessible through the material at hand. The mortuary record of Late Iron Age Norway for example, does not yield as much skeletal material as could be desired if one wishes to carry out an analysis of the relationship between sex and gender structures in a given society, and I will look at some of the implications of this below.

The apparent lack of gendered female graves in the Viking Age mortuary record has often been pointed out (Hofseth 1999:103; Skre 1997:49; Stylegar 2010:71), and a superficial glance at this evidence shows us a demographic dominated by men to an implausible degree: for example in some areas only one in eight graves is listed as female (Hofseth 1999:101). In Vestfold only a quarter of sexed burials are female (Stylegar 2007:82). This is in general accepted as a reflection of prevalent social structures at the time: that men were more in the public sphere, and women belonged indoors, in the private sphere, and that this caused a disparate representation of the sexes in the mortuary evidence (see for example Gansum 1995 for this type of argument). Part of the aim of this study is to question this assumption, and to enquire whether it may rest too heavily on written sources, without sufficient reference to actual archaeological evidence.

The first concern which should be noted is that the majority of Norwegian Viking Age burial evidence has been sexed archaeologically, rather than osteologically (Stylegar 2007:83). In other words, the gender has been determined through certain artefacts found in the grave goods, or a combination of artefacts (Haugen 2009:21). For Viking Age purposes, this means graves with weapons are determined as male, and graves with jewellery, often in the form of oval brooches, are female (Haugen 2009:21; Hofseth 1999:104; Sjøvold 1944:9). There are nuances to this of course: tools are associated with both sexes, although certain items such as textiles working tools are most often associated with female burials. Some weapons can also double as tools, as for example axes, not uncommonly found in female graves, but jewellery and weapons remain as the most trusted gender-deciding artefact groups (Hofseth 1999:104). A number of archaeologists choose to rely on archaeological over osteological sexing even when both are possible (see for example Lucy 1997:154), and some archaeologists will argue that this will give a truer image of the society in question, as it will invariably give access to the image which these individuals wished to project of themselves, of their gender identity rather than the actual sex (Haugen 2009:23). I disagree with this, and would counter this argument with the suggestion that without assessing both the sex and the gender, that is both the physical body and the gender identity, there can be no access to, or insight into, the finer points of gender structures and negotiations. When inferring sex from gender, as is often done when graves are archaeologically gendered, there must be an underlying assumption of a strict correlation between the two categories, which is not always applicable (Skogstrand 2002:111). For example, if dealing with cases of 'cross-dressing', examples of 'third genders'[1], or simply of gender fluidity in transgression of gender roles and females with male trappings or vice versa, the reality of this would be lost to us by only having access to the trappings of gender without knowledge of the sex, and I think our understanding of social structures would suffer as a result. Further, the subtleties of gender could be lost through a lack of understanding of fluid gender roles, if we set out to sex burials strictly on the artefacts which modern values term male and female. 'Gender has as much to do with what we do as what we are' (Skogstrand 2002:121), and as such we cannot be too careful in avoiding stereotypes and projection of our own values when we are interpreting the past. A person's gender identity will often be shaped by their physical attributes: whether this is a result of 'conforming to the norm' of the two sex model, as is assumed to have been dominant in the Viking Age (Solli 1999:423; Svanberg 2003:21), or by opposing it, is of relevance. Further, deviations from the norm must be expected, and a strict reliance on stereotypes of male and female artefacts may detract from an understanding of this.

---

[1] Third gender debates have often drawn on examples such as the Native American *berdache;* most often a man who dressed and lived as a woman, yet was not either a man or a woman, but instead fulfilled a separate role. Eunuchs are another such class who fall outside the 'two sex' structure (Gilchrist 1999:9)

Chapter 1: Introduction

Now, we know that many of the graves from Viking Age Norway have been sexed archaeologically, and we also know there is a heavy majority of male burials, as well as a large number of unsexed graves and a deficit of female graves (Stylegar 2007:63). I will suggest a few potential explanations for this, and will further use this study to explore whether or not it might be necessary to reconsider our acceptance of the established gender pattern in Viking Age burials.

Gendering graves archaeologically will often mean there are ambiguous categories of finds, and 'gender neutral' categories which are found with both women and men. There are also often complicated categories, such as the beads of the Norwegian Viking Age. These are often assumed to have been female, and yet they are known to exist in male graves as well (Johansen 2002:468). It is often stated that a high number, usually more than three, of beads in any one grave means it is female, but there are many instances of women with only one bead, and there are men with more than three (Johansen 2002:469). In female graves, the beads are described as ormanents and indicators of fashion, whereas in male graves they become amulets or artefacts with magical properties (Johansen 2002:468). Beads in male graves are often larger in size than in female graves, and are often referred to as 'sword-beads' (Johansen 2002:471). Although there are some differences in male and female patterns in beads, these are not universal, and there are several exceptions to the stipulated gender pattern rules (Johansen 2002:469), making beads a n ambiguous category in terms of gender determination. This remains a difficult artefact category, as we cannot be certain of gender based on the presence of beads.

Weapons are often considered the ultimate male category (see for example Blindheim 1981d:99), and yet there are examples of women buried with weapons (see Chapter 6 for a further discussion of such examples of fluidity in gendered artefacts). Similarly, there are examples of men buried with 'female' trappings such as textile working tools, which we will also discuss further in Chapter 6 (Lia 2002:306–307). This serves to show the uncertain nature of all 'sexed' finds, and begs the question of whether there is such a thing as a category of finds which belong exclusively to one sex.

A difficulty with archaeological gendering on the basis of weapons indicating men, and jewellery indicating women, is the danger of missing variations in the mortuary record, and thus by assuming these categories are fixed, of only finding what look for (Yilmaz 2005:250).

It has been pointed out that there is a tendency for bias in determining ambiguous graves as male (Arnold 2002:240). In my opinion, the archaeological gendering of graves is often open for projecting our own values on to the past in a way which could be detrimental to our understanding of gender roles. In archaeological gendering, stereotypes often become the norm, and thus there is potential for missing out on the true nature of social structuring principles. It must be remembered that a burial may easily represent an exaggerated image of reality, or even a distorted one with regards to social identity, and this is easy to lose sight of when relying too heavily on archaeological gendering. With this in mind, attention can also be drawn to the fact that there are not nearly enough professionally excavated cemeteries from the Viking Age, and where found, these tend to have a higher number of female graves than what is considered the norm, such as at Kaupang (Stylegar 2007:65). Male markers, such as weapons, are also harder to miss, and rather more noticeable than the oval brooches found with women (Sjøvold 1944:83; Stylegar 2007:83), and this may explain why female graves are sometimes overlooked, particularly in cases of accidental discoveries. Further, we ought to allow for differences in dress through time and space. There are documented examples of female Viking Age graves without oval brooches, as for example Oseberg, and it must be considered likely that women were buried both with and without these. It has also been suggested from Danish evidence that the richest, and the poorest, women did not wear oval brooches (Stylegar 2007:83), and it must be deemed possible that these brooches were an accessory used by only some of the social classes of the Viking Age. And yet, without them, or other forms of jewellery, many archaeologists are reluctant to sex graves as female (Hofseth 1999:1; Hjørungdal 1991:72; Kristoffersen 2000:20; Yilmaz 2005:250).

On the subject of jewellery, Stylegar has pointed out the drop in the number of female sexed burials in the 10th century as opposed to the 9th century, and has suggested this may be due to a change in dress customs, and a tendency to wear less jewellery (Stylegar 2007:82). It could of course also be related to economic concerns, where valuables such as brooches were not deposited, although this would need to be assessed in light of other, temporary, deposits and finds before further assertions are made. In summary, Stylegar sets out a convincing argument that more men were buried with gender specific artefacts that are preserved and can be recovered by archaeologists than women (Stylegar 2007:83). Add to this the suggestion that we may not hold all the keys to understanding the gender coded artefacts of the Viking Age, and that we therefore may fail to see gender structures in graves through a limited understanding of which items were considered 'female', and 'male' and this maps out the basics of the argument which I wish to explore through this study. It is not my intention to question gender–determined graves in the evidence we will be looking at in this instance, but it is important to be aware of the potential weaknesses of the basis of gender determination in order to understand the basis of examining the gender disparity of Viking Age burials. I believe it is unwise to continue to represent gender categories according to modern stereotypes without further questioning, and this appears to me to be doing a disservice to both men and women of the past. Studies which talk of the 'sexual aggression og pagan men' (Jochens 1995:166), or which tell us how Valhalla, one of the realms of dead warriors, is a concept of how 'warriors of the Viking Age expected to be wated on hand and foot' (Jesch 1994:127), are no less harmful in their stereotyping of male roles than are stories which tell us of housebound, hidden women. If we assumed therefore that our understanding of female roles in the Viking Age is incomplete, it follows that this also applies to our understanding of male roles. The line of enquiry which appeared the most obvious to me was that of the representation of gender in the landscape, as I will now proceed to outline.

1.4 Gender expressed in the landscape

A basic premise for this study is that the spatial organisation of landscape carries messages of how the world was structured by the people who inhabited it (Lund 2009:24). Inherent in this is of course the idea that places can signal social variables such as gender, and that the landscape can be seen as a record of social history (Ashmore 2007:260). Again, the following chapter will give a more detailed outline of the history of landscape studies, and here I will merely touch on my understanding of how to best approach culture and social aspects through material remains. Landscape is subjective to the individual and yet at the same time culturally loaded (Thomas 2001:166). At the same time, it can be said that personhood is defined culturally, and to some degree dependent on landscape in the sense of dependency on places is part of cultural coding (Fowler 2008:291). Landscape will influence perception, though cannot be said to determine thought (Tilley 2008:273). In order to make it a meaningful category, we must attempt to unravel the meanings assigned to features in the landscape. Structuring landscape can be a way of structuring the world, and a landscape can thus represent more than just immediate surroundings (Thomas 2001:172). It has been stated that the 'history of human life is about ways of inhabiting the world (Barrett 1999 in Ashmore 2007:259), a quote which highlights the importance on understanding the relationship between people and landscape. Interpretations of landscape often rely heavily on visual aspects (Rainbird 2008:263; Tilley 2008:272), although the 'lived landscape', with an emphasis on experience rather than visual perception, has been held out as an alternative approach by some (as for example Thomas 2001). This may present difficulties, as how you experience landscape is surely culturally coded. The visual aspect may arguably be more approachable as a more unchanging category. I do not believe that experience carries meaning without understanding, and in terms of landscape, this understanding will often come through visual perception. Of course, other senses may play a part in the understanding of one's surroundings (Tilley 2008:272), but an understanding of the 'lived landscape' (Thomas 2001:173) is hard to access without knowing more about the ways of thinking, and ways of structuring meaning of the people who inhabited a specific landscape. The visual

approach at least gives us a tangible means of accessing coded meaning in the past, which can then be used to attempt to access deeper meaning in combination with other material evidence. The emphasis in this study is on the marks left on the landscape by human actions in the past, and consequently there will be an emphasis on the visual aspects of places and areas, as I believe this to be an integral part of the ideas behind where monuments were placed. The visual level must be seen from a human vantage point, in order to reflect how it would have been perceived by past inhaibtants who used landmarks to structure their ideas. Identity and power is often expressed in the use of landscapes, often through the relationships between the living and the dead (Ashmore 2007:264). The Viking landscape, in particular the mortuary landscape, carries to my mind a strong aspect of visually coded meaning: burial mounds and cemeteries seem to utilise landscape in order to manifest meanings and carry culturally coded messages, such as will be discussed throughout this study. Of course, the visual aspect must in turn be interpreted, and may represent a way into understanding the choice of places in the past. To employ visual strategies as a way to understanding the landscape does not mean disregarding the embedded meanings which may be based on a variety of considerations. The landscape can be seen expressing a co-dependent relationship between people and places (Thomas 2001:181), which can help us understand the past. Thus, the strategic use of landscape may play a contributing factor in shaping perceptions and understandings. The perception of meanings embedded in landscape will be a variable dependent on the status, personal history and cultural affiliation of the observer (Rainbird 2008:264), but interpretation of the coding can give understanding of what features meant to different people. It follows that as perceptions of landscape are subjective, thus modern interpretations of landscape will be coloured by modern ideas and thought structures, and so caution is necessary in all interpretations of the past. The suggestion that the use of landscape in the Scandinavian Viking Age had close ties to elements of cosmology, mentality and beliefs for those who inhabited the landscape is important to this study. The premise that the cognitive categorisation of meaning was interlinked with the ways in which landscape was perceived, used and changed (Lund 2009:58) is part of the basic theoretical platform from which I have worked in order to produce this study.

In order to approach the coded landscape in terms of gender based divisions, I will attempt to study the relative topographical positioning of female graves in relation to male counterparts. I believe this is an avenue which has not been sufficiently explored, but which can give us insights easily missed through a traditional focus on grave goods. If we work from the assumption that we ought not assign our own gender

Chapter 1: Introduction

ideologies on the past without questioning, a point which I believe most archaeologists would concede, then it seems clear that this is something we ought to explore further. Dagfinn Skre has argued that Viking Age burial mounds were placed where they were for a reason, and that from the different positioning of graves, it can be assumed they carried different meanings (Skre 1997:38). On the basis that location mattered to the people of the Late Iron Age when they carried out burial rites, it can be suggested that the position of male and female graves may tell us something of social structures.

Place matters, in that a landscape can be seen to be assigned meaning through places, and can be argued to be made up by a series of places (Casey 2008:44–49), and these places mean something to the people who live in relation to them. There is no such thing as a 'non-place' (Thomas 2001:173): a space is created when meaning is assigned to a specific area or feature in the landscape. The landscape can be seen as being made up of meaningful places in which lives are lived (David and Thomas 2008:38).When trying to understand the meaning of a monument, one must also consider the place in which it is located (Jerpåsen 2009:137). If place would have been chosen deliberately, either because it had meaning, or because it could be assigned meaning, this may also be argued to apply to individual burials within cemeteries. By looking at the relative positioning of female and male graves, I believe there may be a way of accessing a different view of the gender roles of the Vikings. Through looking at the physical traits of a location, or place, such as visibility and relative location in comparison to other potentially significant features I will attempt to assess what observable differences there are between male and female graves, if any. If it is the case that male and female characteristics were valued and weighted differently by the Vikings than how they are in our modern society, and perhaps even meant different things from what they do today, and if there is a possibility that archaeology has hitherto relied too heavily on written sources in its attempts to understand the gendered Viking society, then the actual physical location of graves may provide a basis for a more balanced understanding. Alternatively, if it is the case that women were closely tied to the home, whilst their men were out pillaging and trading, then this too ought to be represented in the topographical positioning of the graves. Regardless of the evidence to be discussed it also is but good archaeology to question assumptions and stereotypes and to do so through material evidence.

1.5 An outline of what is to follow

So far this chapter has been primarily involved in describing the theoretical platform from which I have approached the evidence. It may at this stage be prudent to give an overview of what will be covered in the following chapters. As should be evident, Chapter 1, the introduction, aims to give structure and meaning to the following chapters, by outlining my theory and methodology. Chapter 2 will follow on with an introduction to the past research into the main theoretical paradigms and strands with which this study is concerned, in other words it will talk about Viking studies, gender archaeology and landscape archaeology. Chapter 3 aims to provide context to the arguments presented in the study by giving a broader view of the social structures and belief systems of the Late Iron Age, and will therefore discuss the assumptions which can be drawn from the various sources to hand, in terms of social and cultural ideals and reality, and how these can be approached through tangible remains such as landscape and material culture. The main empirical evidence will then be discussed in Chapter 4 and 5. Chapter 4 will be concerned with the Oseberg grave in Vestfold, which belongs to a class of very wealthy, even conspicuous burials, characteristic of the Viking Age. Chapter 5 will examine the site known as Kaupang, also in Vestfold, a site known for its extensive and thoroughly examined cemeteries. As these sites are of a widely different nature, they have been given somewhat different treatment here. The chapter concerning Oseberg gives a more in depth discussion, such as is natural for a single site focus, and which I deemed necessary in order to create a meaningful discussion of the material. Kaupang on the other hand, which has a wealth of burials, aims to give an overview of the material, with a subsequent in depth discussion in Chapter 6. Chapter 6 contains the main discussion of the evidence presented. Finally, Chapter Seven will provide a short summary and conclusion.

Chapter 2. Previous research

This chapter will give an overview of the history of the different theoretical strands contained within this study. We will start off by looking at the history of Viking studies in Norway. We will then examine the archaeology of gender, and past research into gender archaeology, before finishing with a brief discussion of landscape archaeology.

2.1 The history of Viking studies in Norway

Understanding that different social and cultural circumstances will give rise to different interpretations and understandings of the past, is an important point when one wishes to approach the history of archaeology in Norway. At the time when archaeology became a recognised academic discipline, Norway had been under the Danish and Swedish rule for a considerable time and was thus in search for a national identity (Gansum 2004:28). The national romanticism movement involved a search for a common identity which found support in the remnants of Viking material culture (Forseth 1993:2). Archaeology presented a potential link with a past which was romanticised and glorified: Snorre Sturlasson's sagas described the ancient kings of Norway, and Snorre had himself tied the ancient ruling classes of his Sagas to Vestfold. An edition of the sagas was published in 1838 with illustrations of the Viking burial mounds at Borre, and captions that tied these monuments with the ancient kings of Norway (Gansum 2004:29). When the first long ship was found at Borre in 1854, this further cemented the belief in the sagas as a historical source of the earliest kings and queens of Norway (Gansum 2004:29). Not only did this bring to attention a time when, according to historical tradition, Norway was unified into one kingdom, but it was also a time when the nation was a real power to be reckoned with on the international stage. For a country which had not seen real independence for centuries, the Viking Age became a potent symbol of past glory. The ship burials became a symbol of ancient kings, and helped create pride in the Norwegian Viking heritage (Opedal 1998:85). In the words of A.W. Brøgger 'it was a great time and has given us great monuments' (Brøgger 1921:1).

The early days of Archaeology in Norway was largely shaped by influential archaeologists such as Nicolay Nicolaysen, and Olaf Rygh (Sjøvold 1944:6; Lia 2001:11). In common with the general trend of early archaeology in other countries, there was a heavy emphasis on building a chronology based on material evidence, and like most archaeology of that era, it centred around collecting 'antiquities' (Lia 2001:2). This period also saw the formation of the idea that past rituals and beliefs can be accessed through mortuary remains and artefacts (Lia 2001:12), and it can be said that the idea of interpreting social and ritual practices from mortuary remains has been on the archaeological agenda since the discipline's first inception into academia (Lia 2001:33). It was a time of very valuable and exciting discoveries, but perhaps not the best archaeological methods (Sjøvold 1944:6). Some advances were made however, such as when Nicolaysen recorded thorough maps and notes of his excavations at Kaupang (Gansum 2004:45).

The next generation of archaeologists, exemplified by Haakon Shetelig and Gustafson saw a change in legislation which stipulated that all artefacts predating 1536 belonged to the state (Lidén 1991 in Forseth 1993:3). This resulted in a slight shift in focus, away from being mainly about collecting artefacts, and moving more towards a cultural historical approach (Forseth 1993:3). The excavation of the Oseberg mound for example is very well documented, and seems to demonstrate a concern with the bigger picture of the burial and the wider context (Brøgger et al. 1917).

In his time as curator of the national collection of antiquities, Gustafson carried out several high profile excavations, the most famous being the Oseberg ship burial (Brøgger 1921:1). His successor Brøgger moved towards an archaeology which combined the use of the available written sources with the archaeological evidence which was emerging, as exemplified in his 1916 thesis which linked the ancient kings of the sagas to actual burial mounds found in Vestfold (Brøgger 1916; Myhre 1993a:12). The common denominator for all of these academics however, was a marked and explicit interest in the Iron Age, and in particular the later stages known as the Viking Age. Written sources were at the time accepted as historical accounts, and there was a concern with finding the kings and queens described in these accounts in the archaeological record.

Following Brøgger's influential 1916 thesis, the county of Vestfold was the subject of much archaeological interest, perhaps mainly due to the spectacular ship burials which were discovered there, and to the fact that it was popularly held to be where the 'Ynglinga-family' hailed from. This clan of kings and rulers are described in two early written works, 'Ynglingatal' and Ynglingasaga' (Gansum 1997:28), and from this clan came Harald Hårfagre, the king who was attributed with unifying Norway in the Viking Age (Snorre 1943:41). These theories have had a strong hold on the Viking Age archaeology, but it is now considered unlikely that we will be able to locate the graves of the people described in these stories, and that the interpretations which placed any particular king or queen in a particular mound can be seen more as part of the search of a national identity in the 19th century rather than solid deductions of historical fact (Gansum 1997:27). The Ynglinga stories are considered more as myths of origin hailing from the middle ages than as reliable historical fact (Gansum 1997:28; Gansum 1996:9). It is also prudent to add that this is not really of much interest – who was buried where is no longer a

Chapter 2: Previous Research

subject of much importance (Gansum 1996:10), as the focus now sits on understanding social structures, ritual meanings and culture.

A number of works were published in the mould of the archaeology of the turn of the 19th century, perhaps the last noteworthy example being Sjøvold's work on the Viking age in Vestfold (Sjøvold 1944) which followed the pattern of classifying and sequencing finds. After Sjøvold, there is a noticeable lull in the archaeological work connected with the Viking age, easily attributable to the aftermath of the Second World War, and the consequent reaction to the glorification of all things Norse which was prevalent in the ideology of Nazi Germany, and the use of old Germanic symbols in their propaganda which left a somewhat unpleasant association with Viking studies (Gansum 2004:60; Opedal 1998:36).

The next paradigm shift in Viking studies came with the shift in the ruling paradigms of archaeology, with the New Archaeology which emerged in the 60s and 70s in America and England (Stylegar 1995:2). A new focus was put on understanding settlement patterns, and logical positivism abounded. In due course, came a reaction to this positivist view of archaeology, in the form of an increasing dissatisfaction with the limited emphasis it put on cognitive factors, and the tendency to look only at the big picture, disregarding the more local, individual features (Johnson 1999:98). This resulted in what is now known under the umbrella term of post-processual archaeology, lead by influential writers such as Ian Hodder (Johnson 1999:98). These movements can easily be found reflected in Viking studies, as the emphasis moves from the early focus on 'antiquities', to the sweeping generalisations which resulted from the new archaeologists positivist studies on trade links, and more recently to the focus on the individual in the past, on cognitive abilities, and on, as Hodder called it, reading the past (Stylegar 1995:2).

Current approaches to Viking studies are no exception to the prevailing current trend of academic diversity. The arrival of relativism, after the rigid positivism of processual archaeology, has meant that there is plethora of theoretical routes, and an infinite freedom of choice in which theoretical framework one chooses to apply. Along with the focus on social categories, gender has taken an active role in interpretations during the last three decades, and this is the subject discussed in the next section.

2.2 Gender studies

The 'beginnings' or the 'roots' of gender archaeology has often been traced back to Conkey and Spector's influential paper of 1984 (Conkey and Spector 1998). It is worth noting however that by this time, there was already a healthy debate in the Norwegian archaeological community surrounding the significance of gender as a social category (Bertelsen et al. 1987).

At the outset, gender archaeology was marked by a clear desire to redress the image of prehistory where women were either invisible, or at best visible but insignificant (Conkey and Spector 1998; Gilchrist 1999:2).

There is no denying that archaeology is a discipline which has traditionally been deeply coloured by androcentric bias, and the historical dominance of men over women had been naturalised to a degree where it arguably appeared to be the natural order of things (Arnold and Wicker 2001:vii). The traditional subject in archaeological interpretations is the adult male (Fahlander 2006:27). Works such as Man the Hunter presents rather obvious examples of this deep rooted bias, but a short examination of archaeological representations of the past written before the mainstream impact of gender archaeology will often show an image of active man creating civilisation, and passive woman remaining in the background (Arnold and Wicker 2001; Conkey and Spector 1998:16). In these interpretations of the past, women were of course present, but often assigned a static, passive role in social progress, which created a self-perpetuating image where men and male values are more important to the development of cultures and societies than women and female values, an image which has persisted even in our modern western culture (Conkey and Spector 1998:13). Commonly in early archaeological representations, women tend the hearth and the home, they bear children, make pottery or weave and sometimes they gather food (Conkey and Spector 1998:13). But these tasks and roles are made insignificant by the focus on the more active role assigned to male activities such as hunting, warfare and politics, which are deemed more important, and by this assumption women become measured against the male norm (Hjørungdal 1991:64). In short the public sphere was, and to some degree still is, what is deemed relevant and important for the development and progress of human social organisation, and the public sphere is the domain of men, a way of thinking which leaves women hovering on the margins of our interpretations of the past, and by extension they are seen as less important (Conkey and Spector 1998:14; Gilchrist 1999:10). Feminist archaeology has argued that this projection of our own western values on to the past is a form of presentism which can seriously distort our view of the past. The emergence of feminist approaches to archaeology served to highlight the inherent gender bias which permeated what had previously been presented as the neutral science of archaeology (Hodder 2007:27).

The association of women with nature and men with culture is a western prejudice (Lillehammer 2006b:70), which I would like to think has now become a thing of the past. Whether or not this is the case will not be discussed in detail here, suffice to say this was a point of view which permeated archaeological theory for a considerable time, and which often resulted in one-dimensional representations of the social past. Under the influence of this model, the roles of individual agency was neglected, and thus the possibility of understanding more of past gender structures was also ignored

Early gender archaeology can perhaps then be said to have been a search for women in the past, which was closely tied up with the second wave feminism of the 60s and 70s (Gilchrist 1999:2). It is not surprising that the earliest practitioners in gender archaeology wanted to show that there were in fact women in the past, and these women were just as important and integral to the development of complex cultures as were their contemporary men. Out of these ideas grew some rather less reputable strands of theory, founded perhaps on Engels famous citation of the 'world historic defeat of the female sex' (Fuglestvedt 2006:45). Theories such as the goddess-archaeology of Marija Gimbutas and others, and the numerous theories put forward for past matriarchic societies (Fuglestvedt 2006:46; Skogstrand 2002:456) have done very little to further the cause of gender archaeology as a serious study. Alluring though it no doubt is, putting forth theories of past matriarchies seems to me to rather defeat the purpose of feminist appraisals by leaning on studies which are often of a questionable standard, and putting forward theories which do not have sufficient grounding in the evidence to hand (Fuglestvedt 2006:47).

Another aspect of the earlier days of gender awareness in archaeology was expressed in a seeming desire to make women into men (Arwill-Nordbladh 1998:50). This meant there was an emphasis on proving women could have participated in 'male' activities, and showing they were no less active than men. A common criticism of this approach in later years has been that this model of sameness gives no room for different social functions, and that it also exhibits presentism in assuming our modern value-judgements were the same for prehistoric people, and that what is considered important now was what was valued in the past. The emphasis has since shifted towards understanding the variety of gender roles and identities which can be expected in a social setting, rather than fitting men and women into strict roles, either from a stereotypical view of where the different sexes belong, or from a wish to promote equality at all costs (Hays-Gilpin and Whitley 1999:5). It is also important to remember that contemporary concerns will always influence the way we are able to interpret the past, as our own cultural frameworks will invariably influence us. An awareness of this, as well as an understanding that different times and circumstances will give different interpretations of the past will help balance our theories.

Gender archaeology still needs to challenge western views of gender roles, and their projection on to interpretations of past societies, and a feminist standpoint is useful in such approaches (Fuglestvedt 2006:59). However, it does not need to 'find' women in the past, or project ideas of past societies where women take the dominant role. Gender studies no longer mean the study of women, but rather of the complex social structures which form the basis of gender.

In terms of gender studies more specifically concerned with the Scandinavian Iron Age, there is a wide array of studies which have appeared over the last three decades, mainly since the late 1970s saw an increase in gender as a perspective. Interesting articles by Liv Helga Dommasnes (1998) and Grete Lillehammer (1989) have for example focused on the social roles of female farmers in coastal Norway. The earlier days of feminist influence also saw exhibitions dedicated solely to the role of women, such as 'The Strong Woman' of the 1990s, a rather emotive look at the role of women, and their loss of social standing as a new social order replaced the old, in the coming of Christianity (see Lundström and Adolfsson 1995). Criticised for being highly dramatised and arguably overly emotive, the exhibition did serve a purpose in putting focus on the role of women and created a discussion point. Over the last two decades, growing debate has emerged on the role of women in Viking Age society, often based on the written sources available. Jenny Jochens' study of Viking women from 1996 has a detailed interpretation of the women of the sagas (Jochens 1996), and Neil Price has provided interesting views of the religious roles of women with references to both written and material sources (Price 2002). The following chapter will discuss the use of written sources in more detail.

Modern approaches to gender archaeology in Norway tend to be more balanced, and use gender as a structuring category in order to understand social roles rather than wield sharp feminist arguments for the inclusion of women in the past (Pedersen 2008; Fuglestvedt 2006). This is indeed because gender is now a point considered by most archaeologists in their interpretations, and is commonly accepted as a useful approach towards a more balanced understanding of past societies. My concern though is that there are still areas which need closer examination than what they have hitherto been afforded, in this case, the role assigned to women in the Viking Age. It is important to ensure that stereotypes do not influence the popular image of past societies, as will be discussed throughout this study.

Current gender studies in archaeology are diverse, and show influences from third wave feminism, also known as postmodernist feminism. The questions are no longer how do we identify and rectify male bias in interpretations of the past, but how we can approach an understanding of the gender roles and identities of past societies (Gilchrist 1999:13). The current multitude of archaeological paradigms available has seen gender become more incorporated into the mainstream of archaeological research, and it has opened up new avenues of research (Hodder 2001:3). This 'fragmentation of the discipline' as Hodder has termed it (2001:4) ought not be considered a negative, as it means the theoretical approach to the past is more open than before.

2.3 Landscape – finally looking past things

Julian Thomas tells us that landscape archaeology has a long history, starting with General Pitt Rivers and continuing onwards, where the results of an excavation are often contextualised through a defined area (Thomas 2001:165). That's as may be, but the basis for our modern studies of spatial categorisation and the relations between people, material culture and landscape, are concepts and ideas which have emerged during the last 30 or 40 years of archaeological theory (Lund 2009:50). Looking back, there is little mention of 'landscape archaeology' as we know it today until the mid 1980s (David and Thomas 2008:28). Nevertheless, the processual archaeology the 60s and 70s saw a focus on human impacts on and interplay with their physical surroundings, and a move away from single-site focus, and there was a positivist focus on large scale landscape studies (Ashmore 2007:258; Darvill 2008:60; David and Thomas 2008:28). This influence of New Archaeology was in a sense allied with New Geography (Blake 2007:233). The positivist approach to landscape was largely focused on large scale investigations of settlement patterns, and artefact distribution (David and Thomas 2008:28), with an emphasis on proving patterns and settlement theories (Hodder 2007:27). However, with the subsequent post-processual reaction across the discipline which struck root around the middle of the 1980s, there also came a change in the perception and study of landscape, and a subsequent critique of the earlier approaches, particularly in the European and UK archaeology (Ashmore 2007:259; David and Thomas 2008:32). Within British archaeology, an understanding emerged that people and landscape had an interdependent relationship, where landscape shapes the people that live in it, and vice versa. Many post-processual archaeologists have drawn inspiration from philosophers like Martin Heidegger, who presented a phenomenology where body and mind were not necessarily separate, and where the focus was on that individuals experience the world through our senses and our body (Lund 2009:42).

Landscape, as it is often seen by post-processualists, is used for purposes of maintaining and establishing power structures, and the landscape around a group will be experienced differently according to different social groups and individuals (Fowler 2008:296). Phenomenological approaches during recent years have increased the focus on the influence of landscape upon people, and seeing the world as a fluid and constantly changing entity (Lund 2009:53). So, as a consequence of gender, status, social class and heritage, different groups and individuals will be differently located in the landscape, and thereby create a different understanding of it (Bender in Thomas 2001:176). Archaeologists like Tilley put forward phenomenological theories of how to interpret landscape, suggesting that the structuring of space was a way for humans to understand themselves and their place in the physical and cultural room, and that it also plays a part in the creation of social structures (Rainbird 2008:263; Tilley 2008:272). Some also argue that the visual aspect has been given too much importance in landscape studies, and that we ought to experience the landscape in order to understand it (Thomas in Ashmore 2007:261).

Many scholars now see landscape as a way of representing and understanding the world, whilst keeping the awareness that we cannot separate ourselves from the landscape (Thomas 2001:172), and landscape studies over the last decade have focused on individual experiences of landscape (Brink 2008:109). We interpret the world around us through our bodies, and so our understanding of the landscape is necessarily shaped by our experience of it, and how this experience is interpreted by our different senses (Skogstrand 2002:113). The questions often surround the social landscape, and the interdependency of landscape and social understanding (David and Thomas 2008:33). It has also been suggested that perceptions of landscape depends on the status of the person in question (Rainbird 2008:264), as can be imagined in terms of for example monumental power structures.

The question of how the Vikings understood their world in terms of the landscape that shaped them, and which they shaped, has been asked in many different ways since the arrival of postprocessual landscape archaeology. Archaeologists like Dagfinn Skre and Terje Gansum have looked into the significance of burial mounds, and what their presence in the landscape can tell us (Gansum 1997; Skre 1997), whilst Lotte Hedeager has looked into the ritual organisation of landscape (Hedeager 2002:156–183). The last two decades have also seen a significant number of masters papers written on the subject of the Viking landscape (as for example Engesveen 2005; Lia 2001). Cultural historical studies which utilises place names have also played a role in the more recent studies of the ritual Viking landscape, such as Britt-Mari Nästrom's article on holy places and sites in pre-Christian Scandinavian religion (2004). More recently, Lund's (2009) study on Viking spatial organisation has provided an interesting discussion of the ritual meaning of the landscape.

2.4 Conclusion

The sources on a gendered Viking landscape are often less abundant than what one might wish for. Gender, the body and the landscape is a specialised field which has seen some recent interest (Gilchrist 2007; Joyce 2007), but in terms of Viking Age studies of landscape, gender often takes a back seat, or relies on stereotypes with little questioning of the material and of the spatial organisation of the landscape. The woman is too often assumed to have been a housewife, and so a housewife she remains, and a housewife with no social importance at that, whilst the man was a farmer or warrior (Arwill-Nordbladh 1998:45). The above mentioned study by Dommasnes on gender and power in the Norwegian Iron Age for example, suggests looking at grave furnishings and size of the outer burial mound when looking at status in the past (Dommasnes 1998:339), and neglects to mention the relative positioning of the monuments. There has yet to appear a body of literature on the interesting question of gender and the ritual, and indeed the everyday, landscape, and this study will attempt to tackle some of the questions related to this.

The following chapter will aim to establish a platform in terms of belief systems, power and status, aiming to provide some context for the arguments presented later in the study.

Chapter 3. The Viking Age – a wider context

This chapter aims to outline a wider background to the ideas which have shaped the understanding of two major concerns of this study: gender and power structures. In order to do so, I will discuss what is known about the religious beliefs prevalent in Late Iron Age Norway. Further, I will discuss what is known about gender ideals and manifestations of power in the landscape.

3.1 'Religion', belief systems and the ritual landscape

'The deep and sincere heathen religious feeling permeating the whole thought of the nation must be recognised as one of the most important elements of the age, if one is to understand the physiognomy of the Viking age as a whole'
    Shetelig (in Sjøvold, 1944:92).

The quote above illustrates an early recognition of the importance of ritual and religious beliefs in the Viking Age. This could be extended to highlight the importance of understanding ritual manifestations in any prehistoric society. It is perhaps prudent at this stage to define what is meant by 'religion'. The Vikings termed their own beliefs and practices siðr; a descriptive term which applied to their customs and rituals, and in written sources it is referred to as forn siðr, meaning the traditions and customs of the past (Lia 2002:293; Lund 2009:14). These rituals and customs were varied and changing, geographically and between groups of different social standing (Brink 2007:125; Lund 2009:14), and it has been suggested that the terminology 'religion' implies a too homogenous system to fit Viking Age ideas (Brink 2007:105). It was a system of beliefs which permeated daily life (Dommasnes 1994:28; Fuglestvedt 1997:44), and there were not strict divisions between secular and religious spheres as they are known today (Hedeager 1994:28). Cultic centres were found at farmsteads, and the lady and master of the farm presided over rituals within this sphere (Fuglestvedt 1997:44), thus presenting a contrast with later, more uniform and centralised religions.

The Viking universe is commonly understood as composed of several 'worlds': Miðgarðr, where the people lived, Utgarðr lay on the outside of this, the realm of trolls, and in the centre was Asgarðr, the realm of the gods (Lund 2009:59), with Jotunheimen, the realm of giants to the north (Price 2002:50). All these realms were connected by Yggdrasil, the tree of life (Price 2002:50). This model of strict divisions between the worlds has attracted some criticism as being too narrow and clear-cut (Lund 2009:59), but it is at least a working model which can be further developed. As it is not the purpose of this study to discuss religion in further detail, I will accept this model of multiple but adjacent, physical worlds as a basic idea of how the people of the Viking Age viewed the world.

The information which exists on the gods themselves is of course of a problematic nature, being in the form of written evidence set down by people of a different creed, after Christianity had been accepted as the main religion. However, the sources available give us an image of a varied pantheon populated by somewhat capricious gods, both male and female (Price 2002:50). It has also been suggested that the average relationship with the gods would have been of a different nature from the later Christian tradition of adoration and gratitude, as the Norse pantheon of gods required more a recognition of their existence and powers than complete approval (Price 2002:55). Unlike later monotheistic religions, this was not a religion based on salvation, where the ultimate aim was eternal life after death (Steinsland 1994a:24). It was advisable to stay on good terms with the gods of course and these terms would naturally be dictated by the gods. This study will not be particularly concerned with worship of individual gods, but it is worth noting that female and male deities were assigned the same level of authority (Steinsland 1994b:21). Another interesting point is the existence of two groups of gods, the older Vanir, and the younger Æsir (Steinsland 1991:55; Näsström 1995:61). Of the Vanir, the best known are Njord, Frey and Freyja, whilst the Æsir make up the majority of the gods (Steinsland 1991:47).

Aside from the actual gods, there was also a variety of supernatural powers to be taken into consideration. These include the Nornir, or goddesses of fate, Disir, who are always female, and are part god part spirit, and other beings such as elves and spirits of the dead (Price 2002:55). Some of these beings had ritual activities associated with them.

Many recent studies have focused on the ritual landscape of the Vikings. The role of places and landmarks such as woods and groves, waters, manmade monuments and rocks has been given some attention (Näström 2002:53; Løken 2002:269; Price 202:62). Hoards of valuable deposits are often found near boundaries such as water, and also near burial mounds (Näström 2002:65). Natural boundaries abound, and archaeologists such as Mari Østmo have suggested that deposits and remains of ritual activity are found near such occurrences because these were used to confirm the significance of a boundary or a marginalised zone. It is not enough for boundary markers to be merely visible: for them to serve their purpose, they must be known and recognised (Näsman 1994:74; Østmo 2002:187). The landscape has a cognitive aspect, in the sense that we tie our ideas and thoughts to different elements of what surrounds us (Løken 2002: 269–270). These marginalised places also serve a purpose in reinforcing the idea of and existence of safer places, such as the hall of the Vikings – the home cannot be a safe haven unless there are areas less safe with which to contrast it (Lund 2009:65).

Burial mounds are often found near rivers, and there are many cases of ditches dug around the barrows, which may have substituted rivers or streams. Lund suggests this may indicate that water boundaries were used as a separation between the realms of the living and the dead (Lund 2009:257). Rivers certainly appear in written evidence in the role of dividers between gods, giants and people. They are often used to structure and create order in the mythological landscape (Gansum 1999:463). In the Late Iron Age in Norway there is certainly often a correlation between water and burials, as seen with many of the large burial mounds, such as Oseberg and Gokstad which are both placed near a river (Myhre 1993b:32), and Kaupang, where the cemeteries all in some way show relation to water (see further descriptions in Chapter Five).

It is possible that burials played a part in reinforcing such boundaries. After all, graves symbolise the crossing of one of the most powerful boundaries, from the living to the dead. As we will turn to shortly, this may also be related to graves as power-symbols, and as a means of legitimising power by manipulation of the landscape (Gansum 1996:12; Østmo 2002:188). If they were used as reminders of ritual meanings, this could only have added to their power. Østmo and others have pointed to the ancestor aspect of the positioning and importance afforded to monuments which served to tie people to the land of their ancestors by reinforcing continuity and legitimacy (Østmo 2002:188).

The idea of using the landscape to reinforce a message has also been brought forward by Lund, who suggests that the conscious choice to build a new settlement close to an old cemetery may serve to create beliefs of continuity and legitimacy (Lund 2009:8). In short, the landscape can be used to play on what has been termed the collective social memory in order to reinforce authority, or maintain a sense of common identity (van Dyke 2008:278). By demonstrating power in the landscape, the ruling elite may serve to uphold their power by creating a constant reminder to those they wish to rule over, of the difference in their social standing (Bourdieu 1996:42).

The cosmology of the Viking Age shows great diversity, and there does not seem to have been a single belief in a realm of the dead. Instead, there were several options, including Valhall, the realm of Odin, where one half of those dead in battle went and Folkvangr which was Freyja's hall, where the other half of dead warriors went[2]. There was also Hel, reserved for those who died a natural death, or the dead could dwell with Ran in the sea, and also in Helgafjell, meaning holy mountain (Lund 2009:239). Judging by written sources, it was also quite commonly believed that the dead dwelt in their burial mounds (Birkeli 1943:22; Skre 1997:38), though whether or not this prevented them from belonging to one of the other realms of death is uncertain (Lund 2009:239). There thus appears to have been a number of different realms for the dead, and where individuals went is not clear. In addition, there is also a wealth of different burial customs dating from this period (Skre 1997:39). Burial mounds came in widely differing sizes, and are found in locations ranging from large clusters in cemeteries, to freestanding monuments on hills, down in valleys, near roads and in remote regions (Skre 1997:39). Flat graves were also common, some with outside markers, some without (Skre 1997:39). In addition, there are also differences in internal markings, which I will not touch on here. Further, there are several examples cenotaphs, barrows which did not contain burials (Skre 1997:39). From this it can be inferred that the people of the Late Iron Age had a vivid belief in an afterlife for their dead, and it remains an interesting question if this may be reflected in visual remains of the burial rites. An interesting aspect of Old Norse mythology is the presence of an ultimate ending, Ragnarok, where the gods do battle with evil forces, and all perish in the process (Price 2002:51–52). Effectually, this is the end of the world, and no one is spared, which makes the fact that there were such vivid ideas of the afterlife interesting when seen in the light that the afterlife also was finite, and had a predetermined ending (Price 2002:51–52). Voluspå, where this final fate of the world is set out, ends with a few verses which tell of rebirth where the world rises again and the 'worthy warriors' will dwell (Price 2002:52). However, these last lines betray a Christian influence, and it has been suggested that they were not an original part of original Norse beliefs, but rather added as a postscript by someone of Christian faith in the 11th century or later (Price 2002:52).

Leaving aside questions of eternity, and judging from the various aspects mentioned above, it would appear that the landscape often acted as a conveyor of meaning in the Late Iron Age, which adds weight to the arguments put forward in this study.

An interesting thing to note here is the influence of folklore and myths that lived in people's memories in the 19th century. At the time, they were referred to by many names, such as 'giants mounds', 'risegrav' and 'dansar haug', but Nicolaysen recommended they be referred to under the single term 'burial mound'. Omland has argued that this effectively meant Nicolaysen shut off some the lines of enquiry about the mounds, and limited the understanding of their meanings and functions (Omland 2002:34), and I would be inclined to agree with this. That there may have been superstitions worth examining more closely in folk tales seems highly likely. There are early examples of stories which showed a profound respect

---

[2] Sources suggest Freyja chose her half of slain warriors first. In Grímnismál it states ' half the slain she chooses every day', and these would come to dwell with her in her hall at Fólkvangr, meaning field of the army, or field of the people. The realm of Freyja was also an alternative for deceased women (Price 2002:108).

Chapter 3: The Viking Age – a wider context

for the 'mound-dwellers' amongst the people living nearby, and beliefs that these supernatural beings needed to be respected in order to ensure prosperity (Omland 2002:46), and this may give us a hint of part of the symbolic meaning of these monuments in the time in which they were created.

3.2 Gender identities and roles

The Sagas are often acknowledged as the most accessible source for understanding Viking Age gender roles, and the women of the sagas often appear as vindictive and merciless, inciting their men into action by pulling strings from the sidelines (Jochens 1995; Price 2002:111). However, as has been pointed out by many before me, the main bulk of the texts in existence were written after the end of the Viking era, and were based on oral traditions which must naturally have been reinterpreted in the context in which they were told. The texts were recorded in the middle ages, written down by Christian men, and it should not be assumed that they can give us an entirely faithful representation of either history as it was (Gansum 1999:444), or of women's and men's roles in this history (Dommasnes 1998:338; Gräslund 2002:81; Näsman 1994:83; Næss 1994:28; Pedersen 2008:589; Price 2002:111). The texts are now seen as reflections of contemporary world views, rather than true accounts of the Viking Age (Price 2002:52). Texts such as Snorre Sturlason's sagas are quite clearly influenced by a Christian way of thinking (Hedeager 2002:165). It has also been suggested that Snorre played down the importance of female deities in comparison with the male gods, and this may account for the silence surrounding many of them in the written sources (Hoftun 1995:107). We can only ever read male views of the past in these accounts (Tsigaridas 1998:28). However, these sources may still have some value if seen as being anchored in oral tradition. Caution is of the essence if one is to use textual evidence (Lund 2009:24), but when treated with caution, they can be very useful sources for unravelling the past. Among the things these sources can give us, is an insight through mythical elements and explanations to social actions (Gansum 1999:445). In short, I believe written sources may carry considerable value, but that they ought to be used as a frame of reference for archaeological evidence, not the other way around.

The written sources we have to hand are numerous, including the elder Edda, the poems largely accepted as being the most reliable source of information on the beliefs of the Viking Age (Lund 2009:21). There is also skaldic poetry, and the younger Edda, also known as Snorre's Edda, written around 1200 by Snorre Sturlasson as a guide to writing skaldic poetry, and at the same time functioning as an introduction into Old Norse mythology (Lund 2009:18–22). Moreover, there are the laws of the middle ages which are often assumed to include elements from the Iron Age, and of course there are the Sagas as mentioned above (Hedeager 1999:10; Henriksen 1994:49). With this extensive material available, it is of little wonder that the women of the sagas have been a subject of study for many theorists with an interest in gender studies, and perhaps also gives a good justification why archaeologists have tended to accept the image of social structure, including gender roles, gleaned from the written evidence. However, there are concerns with this as will be highlighted below.

An interesting study by Elisabeth Arwill-Nordbladh (1998) discusses how the 19th century popularisation of Viking studies served to cement the image of the Viking woman as influential housewife, through an anchoring in Victorian ideals of home and hearth which was transferred to the Viking Age (Arwill-Nordbladh 1998:39; Stalsberg 2001:70). In popular theory, the domain of women was indoors, and this image is still prevalent in current literature on the subject and is often accepted with little questioning (Arwill-Nordbladh 1998: Dommasnes 1998:337; Svanberg 2003:21). As was discussed in Chapter 2, Viking Age studies was popularised in the 19th century, and subsequently the general framework for understanding the Viking Age was constructed during this time (Svanberg 2003:5), and we must admit the possibility that this has left its mark on our idea of social structures.

As far as it is understood, the social system of the Late Iron Age was based on a system of family, and family honour (Steinsland 1994b:20). The weight of upholding this honour rested on every individual, and was taken seriously by women and men alike (Steinsland 1994b:20). The picture that is often painted of Viking Age society is one of male traders, farmers, seafarers, warriors and craftsmen, with the odd respected and influential housewife thrown in for good measure (Dommasnes 1998:337). However, women can also appear in the form of young unmarried girls, shield maidens, divorcees, widows and sorceresses (Jochens 1996:209).

Evidence suggests that women kept control over their dowry in marriage along with a third of the shared property, that they could inherit land and property, and under some circumstances could participate in the public sphere on the same level as men, but it is generally accepted that their power lay mainly in their influence over their male connections (Dommasnes 1998:338). From medieval laws, which are widely believed to reflect earlier traditions, it is known that inheritance laws in Norway followed family relations through both the male and the female lines, but that the male was often prioritised, at least in terms of land (Skre 1997:48). However, women had rights to property, to divorce and to inheritance (Dommasnes 1998:338; Gräslund 2001:87). The association of women with the hearth and home is based on textual sources, and certain finds which appear to back up women as housewives and bearers of keys, such as keys in wealthy female graves (see for example

Kristoffersen 1999; Svanberg 2003:21). 13th century laws talk of marriage in terms of the woman being given to the man 'to share his bed, for lock and keys' (Gräslund 2001:85), and written sources firmly place the woman indoors and the man out of doors (Gräslund 2001:88). Based on this association of women with the home and the private, they are often less interesting to the historian and the archaeologist, who choose to focus on public displays of power. It has been suggested that the difference in women's and men's approach to power was through the different routes of the public use of authority, which was a male privilege, and the more private influence of women (Dommasnes 1998:342). In common with archaeologists such as Kristoffersen (see for example 1999), I wish to question the value judgement which has traditionally made the home a private sphere, a point which will be discussed in more detail in Chapter 6. At this stage it is sufficient to suggest it is possible that what is considered private now, was more in the public sphere in the past (Gräslund 2001:83). Perhaps we ought not assume that the same value division or indeed the same categories of public vs. private existed in the past. It has also been pointed out that Icelandic sources give us examples of female gydjer, or petty chieftains (Steinsland 1994b:26), and there are persuasive arguments for the similarities in the material evidence in Iceland and Norway to allow Icelandic sources in studies of the Norwegian Viking Age (Østmo 2004:195), if one is to utilise written sources.

I believe it is a fallacy to rely too heavily on textual sources. The gender identities which we are seeking to find in the past may differ widely from the gender attribution which was assigned to women of a rather distant past by historians with no experience of being a woman, or for that matter, a man, in the period about which they were writing. As the following chapters will attempt to show, the mortuary landscape does not reflect the strict division of power which the written sources seem too often to adhere to.

One thing the written evidence can tell us however, is that it is more than likely that the people of the Late Iron Age knew the gender categories of 'man' and 'woman'. Voluspå informs us that human individuals were gendered beings, and that men and women were given the same qualities in life (Lillehammer 1996b:69). It can also be surmised that somewhat different meanings were assigned onto these social categories (Svanberg 2003:21). The question which springs from this is what these meanings were, as well as the correlating value assignments. Christian ideas of gender roles and ideas about sexuality cannot be assumed to have been the ideas of Viking Age society (Steinsland 1994b:26). Texts such as the Lokasenna in which the god Loke mocks and offends the other gods betrays an outsider's view of the sexuality of the Old Norse gods when it mocks Freyja for her promiscuity (Steinsland 2003:131), something which is never listed as a negative in other sources (Näsström 1995:77). Instead, sexuality bears a positive aspect in the myths from the Viking Age, and there is no evidence of ideas of shame or pollution connected with it, other than with male homosexuality which appears to have been frowned upon (Steinsland 1994b:26). There have for example been suggestions that rituals connected with seiðr may have had a sexual aspect (Price 2002:65). In fact, many of the gods openly display and use their eroticism for their own ends, in particular the Vanir, and fertility seems to have been overtly sought and appreciated (Näsström 1994:111). Some gods are known specifically for their aspects of fertility and what might, in want for a better word, be termed promiscuity (Price 2002:108), and extramarital relations seems not to have been uncommon amongst the Viking Age population (Jochens 1995:54).

As suggested by Unn Pedersen, I think the possibility of active female social players must be considered (Pedersen 2008:589). As I will discuss, social fluidity cannot be ruled out before one has examined the material evidence, and as I will attempt to argue in the following two chapters, I believe the archaeological evidence supports the argument of moving away from a heavy reliance on textual sources and early interpretations. As stated earlier, the gender representations which run throughout most interpretations of Viking age society, hail from roots in Victorian ideologies which were read into the textual evidence (Arwill-Nordbladh 1998:39), and good archaeology ought not to accept stereotypes of this kind unquestionably.

3.3 The landscape of power – can we read social status from landscape?

It has been commonly assumed that Viking Age Norway was in essence a society structured by local chieftains and kings. This seems not unlikely, at least for the part of the country with which this study is concerned when we consider the numerous, and often contemporary, large monuments indicating power centres which are dotted around relatively small areas, such as the Borre burials, Gokstad and Farmannshaugen (as discussed by Gansum 1997), and also the remains of power centres such as those examined by Dagfinn Skre near Kaupang (2007a). The question of prevalent power structures in Vestfold during the Viking Age is a theme which has been discussed quite extensively. Early interpretations tended to draw their theories from the Ynglinga-saga presenting the area as under the rule of one influential family (Gansum 1997:28), but in more recent years there have been suggestions that Vestfold was, at least partly, under Danish rule (ibid:33). The exact power structure in terms of nationality or ties with surrounding areas will not be discussed in this study. It is sufficient to state that I find it likely we are looking at an area with a comlex power structure, with room for variety in the internal power structures.

Chapter 3: The Viking Age – a wider context

As has already been made clear, this study will mainly deal with what is perceived to be the upper classes, the higher echelons of Late Iron Age society. The power distinctions with which I have primarily been interested are mainly the divisions within these levels, in terms of social standing associated with birth, land, wealth and occupation. That the Vikings lived in a stratified society will not in essence be questioned here, it is rather the question of gender division between these strata that is of interest.

One of the most conspicuous categories of material remains which may be interpreted as manifesting power, are the barrow-graves dated Late Iron Age. Terje Gansum (1997) has argued the topographical positioning of these burial mounds in the Late Iron Age may have indicated social unrest – that they were a conspicuous display of power, designed as a manifestation of control outwards and social inequalities inwards (Gansum 1997:27). Other interpretations often see the mounds as symbols of legitimacy, building continuity by honouring ancestors, which would help new generations reinforce their claim on land or power (Skre 1997:44; Skre 2007b:363).

'Large' burial mounds are categorised as being more than 20 meters in diameter, and of these there are 147 in Vestfold dating from the Iron Age, most of them in coastal areas (Gansum 1997:28; Iversen, 1999:340). Gansum has commented that they are often placed in 'new' places, rather than showing continuity from the Early Iron Age cemeteries, which he takes as an indication of a change in traditions. He further suggests that Vestfold was not ruled by one powerful family as has been the conventional belief, but rather that it was dominated by conflicting power centres throughout the Merovingian and Viking eras, and suggests this may be a result of Vestfold being under Danish rule at least through part of the Viking age (Gansum 1997:33). The traditional equation of large burial mounds with reigning kings can no longer be seen as applicable when taking the numbers into account (Gansum 1996:11), but that they have some relation with power manifestations remains not unlikely based on their positioning, which often commands a dominating position over the surrounding landscape, and the occurrence of wealthy burials in many of them. The idea that the landscape can be used to signal power and dominate is connected to the layout of monuments and other features, and seems a reasonable conjecture in the case of Viking Age Vestfold.

Further, the actual erection of a large barrow requires a large work effort, and therefore ought to be viewed as a collective effort, representing a collective belief (Gansum 2004:226; Ringstad 1987:71). It ought to be clear, based on the arguments outlined above, that the barrow graves represent visual manifestations of power (Opedal 1998:141). The problem I wish to highlight in the interpretation of this type of power landscape is the suggestion that the burial mounds represent an uncompromisingly male power display, as is suggested by discussions which place female graves on the outskirts of social power (see for example Gansum 1995). Space serves as a stage for gendered performance, and spatial arrangements give meaning through interpretation (Gilchrist 1999:100). The question of whether the landscape of Late Iron Age Vestfold can be said to reinforce a male power sphere will be further explored in the following chapters.

Aside from the widely different numbers of male and female graves which have been gender determined, as discussed in Chapter 1, there are also some widely differing descriptions of the meanings of male and female graves and their positioning. Some, like Gansum, argues that the best known female grave of the Viking era (Oseberg) is anti-monumental, and as such was not part of the public, political sphere, whilst others clearly are monumental and dominate the landscape around it (Gansum 1997:32). Others again, suggest that there is no difference in the location of the burial mounds, their size or contents which indicates that men were afforded a higher status which allowed them universal rule over women (Hoftun 1995:100).

3.4 Conclusion

As has been outlined in this chapter, the cosmology of the Viking Age shows great variety in terms of death beliefs and mortuary rituals. Gender roles appear complex and variable, as does ideas of the afterlife and the gods.

It does appear that rituals and symbolism was to some degree imprinted on the landscape, which will be further explore below. However, I believe it is important to steer away from a reliance on written sources, at least in terms of gender roles and social identities. Historical sources cannot very well be taken at face value when describing mentality and thought structures for people in the past. I believe that by carefully examining material expressions of status symbols and rituals, it may be possible to gain a truer image of past identities. Written sources can be used as an additional source, but always with caution. The next two chapters will proceed to examine the material remains rather than written evidence, to see if there is merit in this approach.

Chapter 4. The Oseberg Burial

This chapter will attempt to open the discussion of a gendered landscape by looking at the actual material evidence we have available. In order to produce a meaningful discussion, I have chosen to look at a focused part of the evidence available, and this chapter will outline what is perhaps the most famous of all Norwegian finds, namely the spectacular ship burial found at Oseberg.

4.1. The Oseberg find

Out of all the known large burial mounds (see Chapter 3) in Vestfold, the Oseberg burial is very possibly the most famous. The discovery of the Oseberg ship burial was in many ways a dream come true for the archaeologists at the time: not only did it yield the richest and most spectacular array of Viking artefacts yet to be discovered, especially rich in organic remains such as wood and textiles (Brøgger 1921:1), it also gave the opportunity to create a potent national symbol at a time of social unrest and uncertainty (see Chapter 2).

The mound was discovered to contain a burial in the summer of 1903, when the local landowner started digging in the barrow and struck woodwork. He subsequently notified Gustaf Gustafson, director of the University Collection of Antiquities (Brøgger 1921:1). Excavation was carried out during the summer of 1904, and did not disappoint expectations of a rich find: the barrow yielded a nearly intact ship, and a spectacular wealth of grave goods. The find has been subject to much study since its discovery, and most works that deal with the Viking Age will touch on it (see for example Christensen et al. 1993; Gansum 1995; Lia 2001; Price 2002).

4.2. Description of the find

The external mound of the Oseberg burial has a diameter of 40 meters, and is estimated to have been up to six metres high when first built (Arwill-Nordbladh 1998:85). It was constructed of quantities of peat, which together with the clay soil contributed to an extraordinary preservation of organic materials (Christensen et al. 1993:7; Sjøvold 1971:10)3. Osteological analysis of the skeletal remains retrieved showed the remains of two women, one in her 50s the other older, perhaps in her 70s (Holck 2009:37 and 67). The bodies had been placed in a ship, aligned north-south with the prow in the south, and the burial chamber positioned behind the mast. Stones had been thrown over the entire ship just before the final stage when the barrow was created and the entire ship covered with clay and turf (Brøgger 1921:3). The ship measured 24 metres long from stern to stern, and was quite broad. It was relatively flat bottomed, and according to experts quite seaworthy, though perhaps designed for calmer waters than voyages at open sea due to its broad shape and shallow position in the water (Brøgger 1921:7). Early interpretations attributed this to the fact it belonged to a woman, and thus was not destined for long sea voyages, though Sjøvold, and later Christensen, has put forward the argument it can be attributed to it being older than other known Viking ships (Christensen 1993d:150; Sjøvold 1971:62).

The inventory is too extensive to be listed here in its entirety, but worth noting is that there was no jewellery, including none of the oval brooches so often described as the definite marker for female graves (Christensen 1993a:58). Some of the more noteworthy artefacts will be mentioned below:

There were several chests found, one of which contained amongst other things textile working tools and a hollow, wooden staff (Christensen 1993c:135). Another wooden staff, with an animal head at one end, often interpreted as a riding whip was also found (Christensen 1993c:126). These two staffs will be discussed in more detail later in this chapter. The grave also contained a selection of textiles, among which were fragments of complex tapestry (Ingstad 1993a:176; Krafft 1955:13; Lunde 1967:1). These tapestries have been much discussed, and are often interpreted in a ritual light, as they are believed to show a procession of sorts (Ingstad 1993b:234). Fascinating though they are, they will not be much discussed in this study, as the study of the tapestries appears to me too large a subject to be included in a study which first and foremost wishes to look at landscape.

Other finds include five wooden animal head posts, beautiful specimens of decorative woodwork (Brøgger 1921:5). It has been conjectured that these head posts may have been used during processions, as they each have a handle by which they could be carried (Brøgger 1917:36; Grieg 1926:362). Several of the enigmatic rattles were also found in here, some in seeming connection with the head posts. These rattles are a bit of a conundrum in the artefacts connected with the Viking Age. Made of metal, they consist of two handles linked by a ring, from which smaller rings hang. Their purpose has been suggested as being connected to equestrian equipment, musical instruments or ritual acts (Christensen 1993c:93). There was equestrian equipment, in the shape of a saddle, and other transport related equipment such as a magnificently carved wagon, four sleighs, and

---

[3] During excavation it transpired that the burial had taken several months to complete, as was evident from organic remains of spring flowers in the earliest layers, and the deposition of autumn apples on the ship (Brøgger 1921:4).

remnants of sails[4]. There was also evidence of animal sacrifice in the shape of 15 horses, four dogs and an ox (Brøgger 1921:6), as well as tools such as an axe, knives and cooking gear (Brøgger 1921:4–6; Christensen 1993a:59).

There are puzzling traits about the Oseberg burial, aside from the obvious questions of who the women were who warranted such a lavish display of wealth. There is for example evidence that the ship was required to be fully ready for travel before interment, as it was found with a mast and what is probably remnants of sails. It also had a full set of oars, some even stuck out through the ships side (Brøgger 1921:6), but only eight were complete, some of the others seemed to have been fashioned purely for the burial, and were not fully finished (Christensen 1993b:82.). Paradoxically, the ship was fastened securely by a rope from its prow to a large rock in the mound, anchoring it to the ground and the mound, and effectively preventing it from sailing away (Arwill-Nordbladh 1998:92).

It was discovered during excavation that the grave had not been left undisturbed – someone had entered it in shortly after the burial was complete, probably within 50 years, by digging a tunnel into the centre of the mound and entering the burial chamber from above (Arwill-Nordbladh, 1998:93; Lia 2002:312). This 'haugbrott', (meaning 'barrow-break'), was by no means an isolated incident, and appeared to have been a rather common custom in Viking times, as many of the large burial mounds from that period show evidence of such intrusions (Lund 2009:244; Myhre 1994:75). However, the purpose behind such an action is unclear. The sagas give us examples of relatives or descendants entering a barrow in order to grapple with the dead to retrieve a powerful artefact. Others have given us stories where descendants seek to speak with the dead to gain access to their wisdom[5]. Modern scholars have put forward a number of different, and in many cases viable theories. It could have been the custom to retrieve powerful artefacts from graves in order to prove your right to rule, or it could have been part of the rituals of death. Another possibility is that it was done by Christians in order to desecrate heathen sacred sites or remove remains to Christian burial grounds, or it could simply be done by grave robbers who sought nothing more than personal gain from their actions (Lund 2009:247)[6]. Interestingly, haugbrott seem to have primarily have happened in graves which contained burials, none have so far been discovered in cenotaphs (Lund 2009: 244. Whatever the reason, the significant factor here is that the haugbrott in Oseberg demonstrates there was no differentiation based on gender on who was given this treatment.

Finally, the dating of the grave was decided by dendrochronology from the intact timbers, which gave the date 834 AD (Christensen et al. 1993:9).

4.3 The barrow's positioning in the landscape

Much has been written about the positioning of the Oseberg barrow. It is placed in the long, shallow valley of Slagen, which runs in a north-south direction (Ingstad 1993b:224). The valley opens up into the fjord around 3.5 kilometres from the barrow, but in order to understand the topography as it was at the time of construction, the higher sea levels of the Viking Age, must be taken into consideration (Gansum 1995:43).

With the sea at approximately four meters higher, a finger of the fjord reached into the landscape, and the shoreline was around 500 metres from the barrow, forming a small bay (Arwill-Nordbladh 1998:85; Myhre 1993b:32). The barrow is situated close to an old river which, although small now, was navigable for a ship the size of Oseberg at the time of burial (Brøgger 1921:2). The valley is closed in by low hills, and in the Viking Age the plain where the barrow lies consisted of marshy wetlands (Ingstad 1993b:224). The surrounding hills were populated by farms, many of which are assumed to date back to Viking Age (Ingstad 1993b:224), and there are relatively high numbers of other burial mounds in the region.

Discussion surrounding the positioning of the mound has often focused on its topographical positioning on a plain, as opposed to some other mounds which take advantage of hills and heights to make them more prominent in the landscape. Brøgger pointed out the similarity of the Oseberg, Gokstad and Farmanns mounds, in that they are all of a monumental size, and positioned on lower lying areas (Ingstad 1993b:226). He went on to conjecture this was because they belonged to a royal tradition and thus had less need for a conspicuous display of power (Ingstad 1993b:226)

Gansum has picked up the argument on the topographical positioning of the large mounds of the Viking age, and has created a thorough argument for the spatial positioning of graves linked to social conditions (Gansum 1995). However, as I will argue, his arguments have serious shortcomings.

Gansum has focused on lines of movement and visibility in the landscape in order to deduct the types of meaning that can be ascribed to Viking Age

---

[4] Gustafson originally suggested this was the remnants of a tent, but Ingstad has argued for it being the sail, based on the thickness of the rope which is found sticking out of the material in parts, and on the positioning of the sails (Ingstad 1982:88)

[5] In cases where written sources tell of such events, the process is often connected with the idea of 'útiseta', meaning a process where a person would sit on the burial mound in the hope of gaining access to communicating with the buried. In such stories, the dead with whom conversation is sought is invariably female (Lund 2009:251).

[6] Worth noting however, is Brøgger's assertion that all known *haugbrott* happed in mounds which have contained burials: there are several examples of empty barrows, but none show evidence of having been broken into, which may support the notion that whoever was behind these acts had some knowledge of the contents of the mounds (Brøgger 1945 in Lund 2009:244).

barrows, and has drawn on levels of visibility in order to set out an argument of social unrest (Gansum 1995). The need to control the landscape as demonstrated by certain monuments may express a deeper need to dominate the people populating this landscape, to assert and confirm control (Gansum 1995:130). The graves positioning in the landscape can reinforce the idea of 'we' and 'the other' which is fundamental to any social structure, where the dead become an exclusive 'we' and the living who view the monuments are 'the others' (Gansum 1995:129). Barrows can symbolise individual power strategies, which break with an earlier, more collective, burial culture (Gansum 1995:130).

Figure 2. Depicts the Raet, an Ice Age moraine ridge which is often judged to have been an important feature in the travel routes of the Viking Age, and it's relation to some sites in Vestfold (Reproduced from Skre 2007a, page 14. Copyright: The Kaupang Excavation Project.)

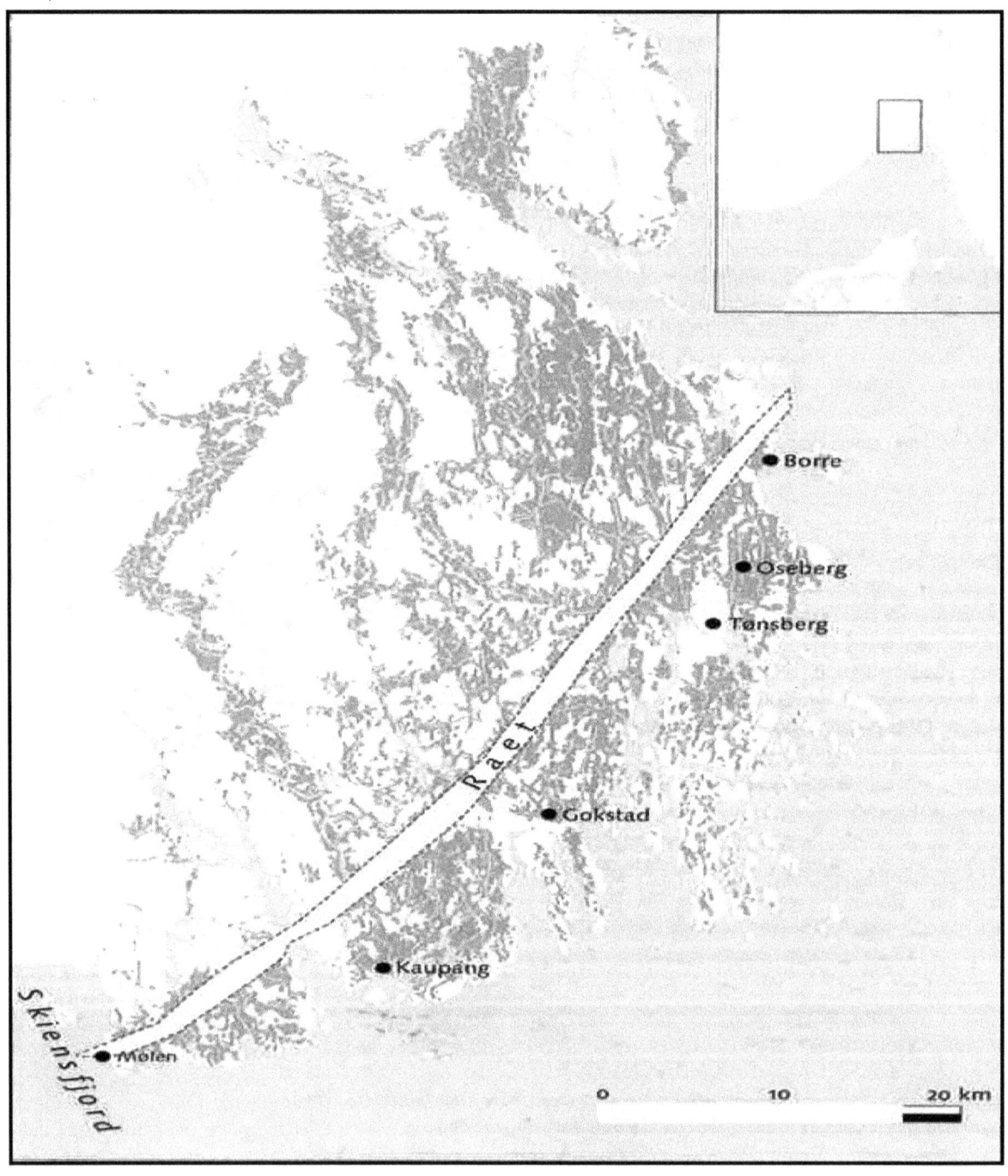

Chapter 4: The Oseberg burial

Gansum describes barrows as monumental or anti-monumental, where the anti-monumental barrows are the ones not placed in high places with increased visibility (Gansum 1995:129). Oseberg is one such, but Gansum removes it even from this category by pointing to the limited visibility over its surroundings from the grave itself (Gansum 1995:129). In the case of Oseberg, Gansum lifts it away from other similar graves and discusses it in isolation. He describes the area as isolated from passing travel, and describes it as a destination rather than somewhere you would pass. This central argument appears to be contradicted in his description of the grave's positioning: although visibility is arguably somewhat limited from the grave, it is highly visible from the surrounding hills. In terms of travel near the grave, the river was passable for ships of a good size (see above) and there was a road which ran along the ridge of one of the flanking hills (Gansum 1995:212). In addition to this, its position in relation to Raet, (or the Ridge) is at a similar distance as both Kaupang and Gokstad (Skre 2007a:14), as can be seen below in Figure 3. This ridge is a large moraine which runs SSW to NNE a little removed from the coast throughout Vestfold, and it represents one of the main overland travel routes of the Viking Age in that region (Skre 2007a:14).

Figure 3. The Oseberg mound seen from a distance. Photograph taken March 2010.

Figure 4. View from the Oseberg mound. Photograph taken March 2010

If the higher coastline, and this the closer proximity to the fjord, is taken into consideration, as well as the numerous surrounding farms, it seems clear to me that it is too simplistic to dismiss Oseberg as a site which did not dominate its surroundings. Its sheer size, and prominent positioning on the flat plain, must have made it a natural point of focus for local residents and travellers alike. It certainly forms a focal point for visitors to the area today, drawing attention to itself by its size and clearly visible location, see Figure 4 for a view in to the mound.

Interestingly, Gansum separates Oseberg and Gokstad in his interpretations. The Gokstad mound housed another spectacular ship burial with the remains of a large man in his 40s who, based on the injuries evident from his skeleton, is believed to have died a violent death (Gansum et al. 2008:4), excavated some 20 years before Oseberg (Bakken 1959:5). The Gokstad burial has been given a date of around 900 AD (Myhre 1993c:43). Although the two have very obvious similarities in their positioning, both being placed on the bottom of a valley, near a river, and within a similar distance from the fjord (Myhre 1993b:29–33), Gansum highlights Gokstad's travel links, and discounts Oseberg's (Gansum 1995:218). He also describes Oseberg as the only one of the large barrows which lacks visibility and exposure, even though Gokstad is found in a similar topographical location, and gives a very similar impression of commanding a good view of

Chapter 4: The Oseberg burial

the surroundings, but being slightly limited by nearby hills: see Figures 5 and 6 for a view from the two respective mounds. His interpretations set Gokstad out as being the monument over a more modest king, one whose power was asserted and accepted and whose descendants did not need to use his burial as a strategic power display. Oseberg on the other hand, he suggests may have been a ritual deposit, even a religious sacrifice (Gansum 1995:221–223). Although Gansum's ultimate self-professed goal, to open up discussion for more alternative interpretations than what has previously been accepted, is admirable, I believe he has been too hasty in classing Oseberg as being outside the conventional power sphere. I also believe he has failed in what he professes as important: that even though the past is created in the present, we should avoid projecting our own ideals on to it (Gansum 1995:9).

It is easy to brush aside a female grave as an anomaly, and this seems to be just what he has done, rather than take up the question of where these women fitted into social power strategies. It appears obvious to me we cannot dismiss this grave as a religious offering on the basis of its slightly withdrawn position if we do not do the same for other graves in similar topographical positions. I believe more would be gained from admitting Oseberg into the arena of social power and discussing it on the same lines as the other large graves, or at least by applying the same criteria for interpretation as we would for any other grave, regardless of the gender of those interred.

Figure 5. View from the Gokstad mound. Photograph taken March 2010

I believe it must be assumed that the large burial mounds of the Viking Age were potent symbols of power, judging by their wealth, position and numbers. A symbol gains its common association and hence its importance, by being repeated, and by being seen to be repeated by the people who are influenced by it (Kobylinski 1995:14). In short, a symbol can only make sense if we have a context in which we can see them (Schjødt 1995:22). This, I believe, speaks against lifting Oseberg out of the context of the other large barrows of its area and time. As a symbol, it must have been read, and in order to be read, it must have a context. That context must, by logical deduction, be other barrows like itself, and we must therefore treat these monuments as manifestations of the same ideals.

Oseberg does not utilise height to dominate its surroundings in the same way as for example the Borre or Haugar mounds do (Gansum 1996:13). But I would suggest this may be for the reason Gansum has suggested for Gokstad – that the burial belongs to a calmer social culture than these other, more prominent features. It lacks the need for demonstrative power, and does not have to 'put itself out there' to the same extent as certain other monuments. Judging from the evidence available, it is widely believed that Vestfold was not under the rule of a single ruling family, but rather that it was divided into several smaller fiefdoms (Gansum 1997:33), as detailed in the Annales Regni Francorum, which speaks of the area as populated by one people with several rulers (Gansum 1996:14). Other barrow graves are interpreted as manifestations of this varied power structure, as monuments raised over chieftains or minor lords. Is it inconceivable that Oseberg was part of the same power structure?

4.3 The Oseberg women

It is somewhat curious that to this day we still talk about the Oseberg Queen, when there were in fact two women found in the ship burial. As mentioned above, the relative status of the women has often been discussed, but the possibility of them being of the same social strata has rarely been suggested. The belief in one as the queen and one as the sacrificed slave may originate in the 'eye-witness' account which has survived in the writings of Ibn Fadlan of a Norse burial along the Volga in the 10th century (Warmind 1995:131). However, as will be discussed in Chapter 6, I do not believe this can be used as a very reliable source of information. Persuasive arguments have been but forward over the years arguing for which of the women was the one who merited such a grave (Christensen 1987:8). There is in actual fact no material evidence of their differing social class that can be gleaned from their attire (Ingstad 1982:94) from the grave goods, or the skeletal remains (Holck 2009:32–67). Further, there is no sign of violence on either skeleton (Holck 2009:62), as might be expected if one was a slave: a human sacrifice is likely to have died a violent death. The younger woman displays a broken collarbone, but this had started to heal, and cannot be connected with her death. There is evidence the older woman died of cancer, and the younger may have died from a brain tumour, as can be suggested from thickened areas in her skull (Holck 2009:59-62). As it is so hard to differentiate them in terms of social standing, and as there is no evidence of a violent death for either, I believe there is a strong possibility that they were of a similar rank, and suggest the burial ought to be studied on those terms until anything can be constructively argued for in favour of one or the other.

Hardly guessing the influence and impacts of his tentative guesses, A.W. Brøgger put forward a suggestion that the Oseberg lady may have been none other than Queen Åsa described in the Ynglinga stories, part of the formidable Ynglinga-family (Brøgger 1916; Pedersen 2008:585). His suggestion proved to take a strong hold of archaeological theory surrounding the Oseberg burial, and even to this day some will draw on this theory, even though there have been strong doubts about the reliability of Snorre's Ynglingasaga as a historical source for several decades (Gansum 1996:9–10). One central weakness in this argument is that it relies on the necessity to explain away a female power symbol on the scale of Oseberg – the ship was after all a male symbol of power and not associated with women before the discovery of Oseberg (Arwill-Nordbladh 1998:113; Synnestvedt 2002:130), and the admission of females into this inner circle of ship burials would mean a certain revision of ideas which may have met with some reluctance. Therefore, interpreting the burial as that of Åsa can be seen to safely tie this female power symbol to male relations, making her into a specific historical figure, rather than symptomatic of a more equal gender and power structure than what would have seemed natural to the prominent archaeologists of the previous century. Further, the theory pushes the Oseberg lady into the margins by making her the wife of a Viking, and mother of another one – it removes her identity and defines her in terms of her male relations in a way which detracts from the obvious display of power so clearly manifested by the grave (Arwill-Nordbladh 1998:113). However, the date of 834 AD given by dendrochronology has safely discounted the possibility of the Åsa theory (Pedersen 2008:586), and this can therefore be left behind. Having said that, it is a theory which has left a deep mark on interpretations of the burial, as can be seen in more recent texts (see for example Christensen 1987).

Other interpretations have ranged from portraying the lady as a Danish princess who had been sent in marriage to a Norwegian ruler (Skre 2007c:467), a religious figure, for example of priestess of the goddess Freyja, or a nameless queen (Pedersen 2008:586) often connected with one of the nearby farms (Ingstad 1993b), or even a religious offering (Gansum 1995:134).

Chapter 4: The Oseberg burial

A common trait for many of the interpretations surrounding Oseberg is that it removes the women from the sphere of direct political power (Pedersen 2008:586), placing them firmly in the domestic sphere, as wife of a powerful man, or in a ritual context removed from the public sphere. Domesticating theories highlight the woman's role as a housewife, wife to a powerful and wealthy husband, and points to her kitchen equipment and textile tools as examples of her female pursuits (Brøgger 1921:4; Christensen 1992:5; Grieg 1926:363). As Arwill-Nordbladh has rightly pointed out, a fully equipped kitchen is commonly seen in ship burials (Arwill-Nordbladh 1998:100), and thus ought not to be tied to the identity of the individuals buried at Oseberg any more than it is in other graves. One way of thinking which affords the women a more active role has been put forward in the suggestion they gained their high status through textile production (Synnestvedt 2006:127). This relies on the idea that women in the Late Iron Age could gain status

ASIKRIR, meaning 'Sigrid owns this' (Christensen 1993:76). Of course, this name may not apply to either of the women, and even if it does, a detached name gives us no real insight into the identity of the deceased. It is nonetheless an interesting detail, which ought to be mentioned in the discussion of the women's identity.

What I believe must be realised here is that women who held, and used, power in the Viking era was not unheard of, and not impossible, or even unlikely. There is nothing very dramatic in suggesting the Oseberg women may have been active political players, and archaeological evidence supports such a belief. In order to approach an understanding of the individuals who were buried at Oseberg, as well as the social and political sphere in which they lived, I believe we need to keep an open mind, and possibly look at a combination of possibilities.

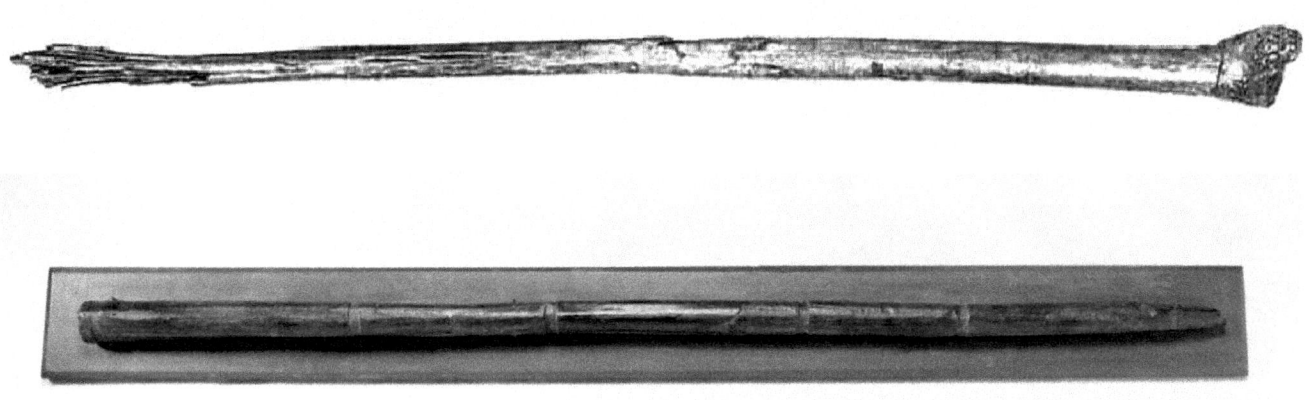

from weaving (after Ingstad in Synnestvedt 2006:131; Gräslund 2001:96–97), and also on the association of weaving with magic which occurs in some of the written source where women are known to 'weave fates' (Synnestvedt 2006:139). Although this interpretation has the virtue of putting the Oseberg women more firmly in the public arena, I would be cautious in suggesting that this level of wealth and status was easily accessible by craftspeople. Christensen in his 1987 article suggested a more powerful stance for the 'Oseberg queen', when he suggested her wagon may have been used for political purposes (Christensen1987:5) and suggests it is unnecessary to tie the lady of Oseberg to historical sources, as she stands out on her own as a wealthy and important individual (Christensen 1987:9). However, his interpretation is too closely tied to the idea of her as a traditional, housebound housewife, and does not dare put her in the light of an independent individual.

There have been two runic inscriptions discovered from the burial, both of which are rather unclear. One reads LITILUISM which has been interpreted as 'man knows little', and another found on a bucket stating

Figure 6 and 7: The two staffs found in the Oseberg ship (reproduced with the permission of the Kulturhistorisk Museum Universitetet i Oslo © Kulturhistorisk museum, Universitetet i Oslo).

Much of the grave goods are things which can be connected with ritual activity, such as the rattles, the animal posts and the tapestries which seem to show ritual proceedings (Pedersen 2008:587). It is possible to take the possible ritual link a bit further: The role of women in Viking cultic activity has been discussed from a relatively early time (Price 2002:61). It was Freyja who was the goddess of seiðr, or of magic, and it was women who took the role of Volur, the practitioners of this art, although the Viking's relationship with this art was somewhat ambiguous, they seemingly feared it and admired it at the same time (Price 2002:113). This is perhaps not surprising when you consider this art supposedly gave powers of knowing the future, but also the powers to inflict death or cause misfortune, even to stealing people's power or minds (Solli 1999:400). At the same time, it could be used for gain, to increase fertility, or to advice on what course of action was the wisest in a given situation (Solli 1999:400). The term 'volve' translates to 'staff bearer', they were travelling women, recognised by the staffs that they carried[7], professionals in their craft who received payment for their services (Price 202:113). Neil Price's interesting argument sees staffs in female burials as indicators of cultic power, and he has drawn on a number of persuasive examples in order to back this up, dealing with both the metal staffs commonly interpreted as 'meat spits' and also wooden staffs (Price 2002:179–187). If we return to the odd wooden, hollow staff found inside a chest in the burial chamber at Oseberg, and also the wooden staff with an animal head commonly interpreted as a riding whip, this theory becomes relevant. Figure 6 and 7 below illustrates these two staffs (see above).

The religious interpretation of Oseberg as a sacred site has often used the name itself, as a version of 'hill of the Æsir' where' berg' means hill, and Ose becomes a genitive of the name of the gods, Æsir (Ingstad 1993b:226). It may be unsafe to base too much of the argument on this, as there is no certain information of what the name was in Viking times, nor of which farm Oseberg belonged to in those times (Ingstad 1993b:231). However, this additional evidence is not necessary in order to conjecture that it should be considered possible that religious power could be linked with social power, and that the Oseberg burial could be the result of one or two such figures of authority. Women were the known practitioners of seiðr, and so it does not seem unlikely that a figure of authority would capitalise on this and bring ritual aspects into their role to strengthen their standing and power, although I will argue against allowing this as the only avenue to power and influence in Chapter 6.

4.4 Conclusion

The next chapter will discuss a site of a different nature from the Oseberg, with its immense wealth and singular position in the archaeological record, before progressing to a
combined discussion of the two. What I wish to emphasise at this point however, is that although Oseberg is the only known female grave out of the monumental large barrows in Vestfold, I do not think this means it ought to be pushed into a role removed from the public sphere of power. If its immense wealth and elaborate ritual aspects alone is not enough to grant it was the grave of a politically visible individual or individuals, its positioning in the landscape, similar to other known graves which are afforded the rank of chieftain, ought to tell us that we are dealing with someone who was part of the ruling elite, (though perhaps a more secure elite than those who used their monuments to shout out loud their position and power over the landscape). Gansum's arguments (1995), if applied a little differently in the case of Oseberg from what he proposes, gives us a picture of a varied landscape of power, where some chieftains or leaders were more secure in their power than others, and this can be seen reflected in the landscape.

As a final note to this chapter, judging from the male to female imbalance of excavated large mounds of Vestfold, some weight is given to the image of a society where men were more likely to gain the highest positions of power, and that women were more often given the position of supporting actor. But this does not mean it can be assumed to have always been so, and we must allow for individual agency and varying circumstances. I believe Oseberg testifies to this, and that this grave must be allowed into the public sphere. With this comes the possibility that the public was not a closed arena for women, and this will be further discussed in Chapter 6.

---

[7] See for example Hedeager for a description of Torbjørg the volve: she carried a staff, wore gloves of cats fur and carried her magical instruments in a leather pouch in her belt (1999:74–75).

Chapter 5. The cemeteries at Kaupang

As with the previous chapter, the aim in this chapter is to further examine the topographical position of burials in the context of gender and social roles at the site of Kaupang. Kaupang is a site rich in burial evidence, and due to a long history of archaeological interest in the area, it has been well documented. I will build on previous research in order to see if anything can be surmised in terms of social influence and significance based on the positioning of known and excavated graves.

5.1 The Kaupang case

The site of Kaupang is located in the parish of Tjølling, in the Larvik area of southern Vestfold (Tollnes 1981:17). The area is now commonly assumed to be the kaupang in Skiringssal described by the traveller Ottar in the late 9th century, where it was described as a busy port and trading place of consequence (Blindheim 1995a:10; Pedersen 2000:25; Skre 2007:13). [8]

Kaupang is believed to be one of the 'earliest towns in Scandinavia' (Skre 2007:13), and is thought to have been founded around AD 800 and remained a busy town until the mid-tenth century, when it was abandoned (Gansum 1997:37; Myhre 1993b:25; Skre 2007:13).

Archaeologically speaking, the site consists of a large area called Svartjorda, which was the habitation and production area, as well as several nearby cemeteries and farms from the Viking Age (Skre 2007:13). The argument for it having been a trading and production centre is backed up by finds of imported goods and coins, the existence of a harbour, as well as evidence of production of different goods (Pedersen 2000:11; Tollnes 1981:17 and 23).

In terms of excavation history, the first archaeological examinations at Kaupang were carried out by Nicolay Nicolaysen in 1867 on the barrow cemetery of Nordre Kaupang (Heyerdahl-Larsen 1981:47). Further excavations were carried out between 1950 and 1957 by Charlotte Blindheim and her team (Blindheim et al. 1981; Blindhem and Heyerdahl-Larsen 1995). [9] At this time, the flat grave cemetery at Bikjholberget was examined, along with parts of the habitation area. Blindheim's team also did trial excavations in Nicolaysen's old area. Blindheim was succeeded by Skre as leader of the Kaupang project, and he has directed further investigations in the area (Skre 2007a). As is evident, Kaupang has seen sustained archaeological interest over the last 150 years, and remains a subject of interest and potential study today.

Most writing concerning the mortuary aspect of Kaupang have dealt with the site in terms of four large concentrations of graves: Lamøya, Bikjholberget, Nordre Kaupang and Søndre Kaupang, although more recent research has suggested that there may be several other, smaller concentrations of burials in addition to these larger ones (Stylegar 2007:65). In the following pages, I will look at Nordre Kaupang, Lamøya and Bikjholberget. Nordre Kaupang consists of a main part, with a few graves clustered south of this, which Frans-Arne Stylegar has suggested is a separate cemetery, Hagejordet. As will be discussed below however, I have chosen to focus on this as one site. Lamøya and Bikjholberget will each be discussed in separate sections. The last of the large cemeteries, Søndre Kaupang will not be discussed in this study. This is because the information available for the site is incomplete, and there is no map or detailed notes (Heyerdahl-Larsen 1981:57). Thus, the exact positioning of the graves cannot be known, as they have been removed from the landscape (Heyerdahl-Larsen 1981:59). Unfortunately, without extensive knowledge of the location of the graves, this site can bring nothing of value to our discussion.

5.2 The Kaupang Landscape

The Kaupang area encompasses the two farms of Nordre and Søndre Kaupang, though in the Viking Age there were four sizeable farms in the nearby area, Huseby, Guri, Bjønnes and Østby (Tollnes 1981:17). To the south, Kaupang borders on the Viksfjord, part of the Larviksfjord (Tollnes 1981:17). The inhabited area, and the surrounding cemeteries, is located close to Raet, a large moraine ridge dating from the last Ice Age, which represents one of the main overland travel routes of the Viking Age in Vestfold, as seen on Figure 2 (Tollnes 1981:17). As with all coastal sites from the Later Iron Age, the higher coastal line of the past must be taken into consideration if we wish to gain an understanding of how the landscape appeared to its Viking Age inhabitants. Lamøya, now a peninsula, was then an island, and the cemetery of Bikjholberget jutted into the fjord opposite this, see Figures 8 and 9. The fjord also jutted in to the area where the cemetery of Nordre Kaupang lies today, creating a shoreline running along it (Tollnes 1981:19). Setting aside the coastal line changes, the landscape of Kaupang has not seen any major changes since the Viking Age, although changes in vegetation and agricultural activity must account for some differences in terms of visibility and accessibility of open views. It can perhaps be surmised

---

[8] Due to its description in written evidence, previous research has often focused on confirming its identity as a historical place (Skre 2007:13). 'Skiringssal' was referred to in several documentary sources between AD 890 and 1300, as a place comprising an urban site, as well as a royal seat, which was credited with cultic importance (Skre 2007a:13)

[9] Blindheim was incidentally the first woman archaeologist to direct a large-scale excavation in Norway (Dommasnes, Kleppe, Mandt and Næss 1998:113).

Figure 8. Reconstruction of the Kaupang area as it would have appeared in the Viking Age (Reproduced from Skre 2007a, page 15. Copyright: The Kaupang Excavation Project.)

that in a time of a sizeable population[10], industrial activity and agriculture, the landscape would have appeared more open, with less vegetation. I believe therefore that an assumption of increased visibility ought to form part of our understanding of the Viking landscape. A reproduction of the landscape as it would have appeared in the Viking Age is included below, in Figure 8. The burial areas are marked in darker grey. The settlement area can be seen on the flat bay area, between three of the main cemeteries, and overlooking the fourth.

As would be expected from its assigned status as a busy trading port, the site possesses clear lines of communication with outside areas.
The lines of communication coming into the town include the overland routes, determined by the lines of Raet, and it is thought travellers would approach the town from the north. The waterways were along the river Numedalslågen, and of course the sea route via the fjord (Tollnes 1981:32).

The landscape is shaped by visual lines fenced in by boundaries created by the low-lying hills. The hills surrounding Kaupang form a visual line running south west to north east. Another line runs along the Bjønnes hills, in a northwest/southeast direction. We find burials placed in between low-lying hills, hidden as it were from the general view, at Lamøya. Bikjholberget appears more visually obvious, as do the barrows at Nordre Kaupang. Figure 9 below gives an overview of the positioning of the graves and cemeteries.

Landscape is never merely neutral surroundings (Gansum 1997:31). At Kaupang especially, I believe it is apparent that place itself matters: there is evidence of contemporary, yet widely different burial rites, all tied to the same town, which are expressed in different topographical settings. The different cemeteries show different dominant traditions in terms of preferred modes of interment, but they were coexistent, all yielding dates from the end of the 700s until the mid-900s, creating a life span of 150 to 200 years (Blindheim 1995a:13). In common with the general trend of Vestfold's Viking Age graves, there is a lack of burials dated later than c. 950 AD (Stylegar 2007:82).

What I believe is crucial in the understanding of the landscape of Kaupang, is that the inhabited area is surrounded by burials. Only in the west were there no graves, and here the area is closed off by the Kaupang hills (Heyerdahl Larsen 1981:65). The inhabitants must have had a constant awareness of the dead, and it can be presumed that this living with the dead shows that importance was afforded to the continuity of tradition and the family.

---

[10] With an estimation of between 200 and 500 people permanently settled at Kaupang, this must amount to a sizeable community (Stylegar 2007:65)

Chapter 5: The cemeteries at Kaupang

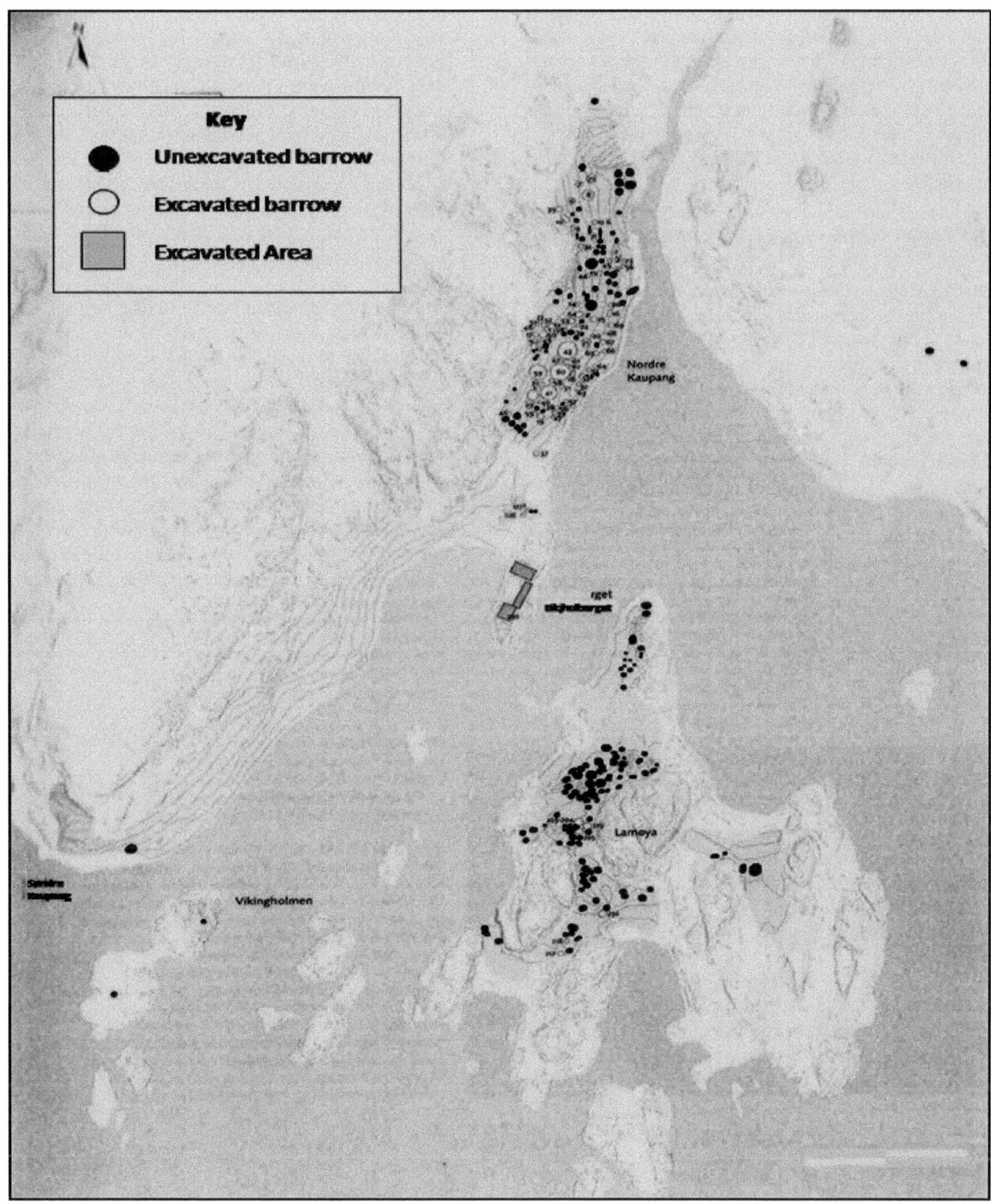

Figure 9. Map of the Kaupang cemeteries (after Stylegar 2007. Reproduced from Skre 2007, page 67. Copyright: The Kaupang Excavation Project.)

On a similar note, any traveller wishing to approach the trading place would pass either through or close by these cemeteries, either on land or by water.

None of the graves at Kaupang appear to have been solitary monuments, and they are not placed in exposed and dominating positions. Nonetheless, with a settlement surrounded by graves, local inhabitants and visitors must have had a constant awareness of the surrounding graves, and it can therefore be said they were imposing to no small degree, though not monumental.

There is quite a high proportion of known female graves from the Kaupang cemeteries, compared to the rest of Norway, and indeed to the rest of Vestfold (Hofseth 1999). Whether this is a reflection on the high proportion of professionally excavated graves here, or whether it is a reflection of the actual burial customs of the time is a crucial point, which we will return to in the discussion in Chapter 6.

In the sections below, I will discuss the cemeteries in turn, focusing on issues of location and topography. My justification for dealing with the mortuary traditions in terms of sites is the clear differentiation in burial customs which has been observed between the differing sites, which suggests to me that they belonged to different, though most likely not conflicting, traditions.

5.3 Nordre Kaupang and Hagejordet

Nordre Kaupang, along with Søndre Kaupang, were the first of the cemeteries to be archaeologically excavated. In 1859 Nicolaysen surveyed of the area, and registered 'hundreds of mounds' at the site of Nordre Kaupang (Pedersen 2000:10; Stylegar 2007:69). In 1867 he returned to excavate, and concentrated his efforts on Nordre Kaupang, where he at that time registered 120 burial mounds (Blindheim 1981a:73). Of these he excavated 71, and found archaeologically datable artefacts in 35 (Blindheim 1981a:73). Nordre Kaupang is by far the largest cemetery found at Kaupang, and the graves excavated by Nicolaysen were cremation graves in barrows, the outside dimensions varying in size and shape (Blindheim 1981a:47). During the course of his work there, Nicolaysen had a map created of Nordre Kaupang, along with notes for the barrows he excavated, all of which have been used extensively in later research.

Niclolaysen's map shows a large site, positioned in a north-south direction between the two hills (Bjønnesås and the Kuleås), and bordering in the north on a stream, the Guribekk (Heyerdahl-Larsen 1981:50). Due to modern agricultural activity, it is impossible to know the true extent of this site (Heyerdahl-Larsen 1981:50), but it has been conjectured there may have been around 260 barrows originally (Stylegar 2007:77).

Topographically, Nordre Kaupang is situated differently from the other major sites at Kaupang. As Skre has pointed out, it is located on the strip of land that runs from the settlement towards the inland areas of the north, and does not address itself outwards to the fjord in the same manner as Bikjholberget or Lamøya (Skre 2007b:380–381). The graves are clustered around the road leading from Kaupang, possibly to central parts of the Skiringssal complex. This 'Skiringssal' was presumably an important centre in the area, and Skre has surmised that the administrative centre, including the hall, is found at the Huseby farm inland from Kaupang (Skre 2007b:383). The hall was in the Viking Age a potent symbol of central power (Hedeager 2002:162). Based on the difference in its positioning, and the above mentioned communication with the road, Skre has argued that Nordre Kaupang was the cemetery used by the chieftains and landowners of the nearby area (Skre 2007b:382). Skre's overall arguments for a power centre at Huseby will not be further discussed here, as this lies outside the topic set for this study. However, topographically the arguments for Nordre Kaupang as slightly removed from the town make sense. The graves are placed between the hills and a finger of the sea, which jutted in on the site in the Viking Age, but they lack the direct exposition outwards to the sea which other sites have, as well as their direct communication with the town. Nordre Kaupang is set apart from the other cemeteries in this lack of close ties with the town itself – the other cemeteries are in direct visual communication with the town, which may indicate a closer connection with the immediate concerns of the town.

Significant to the spatial understanding of this site, is the fact that in order to approach the town, a traveller by land would have to pass through this massive barrow cemetery, which may imply that a level of dominance over those who passed by was sought by the builders of the barrows (Lund 2009:231). In terms of visibility, these barrows did not make use of heights or hills in order to dominate their surroundings, positioned as they were by the foot of the Kaupang hills, overlooking nothing but a strip of the fjord. It is seems clear to me that their visibility was reliant on the road, the overland approach to the market place, illustrated below in Figure 10.

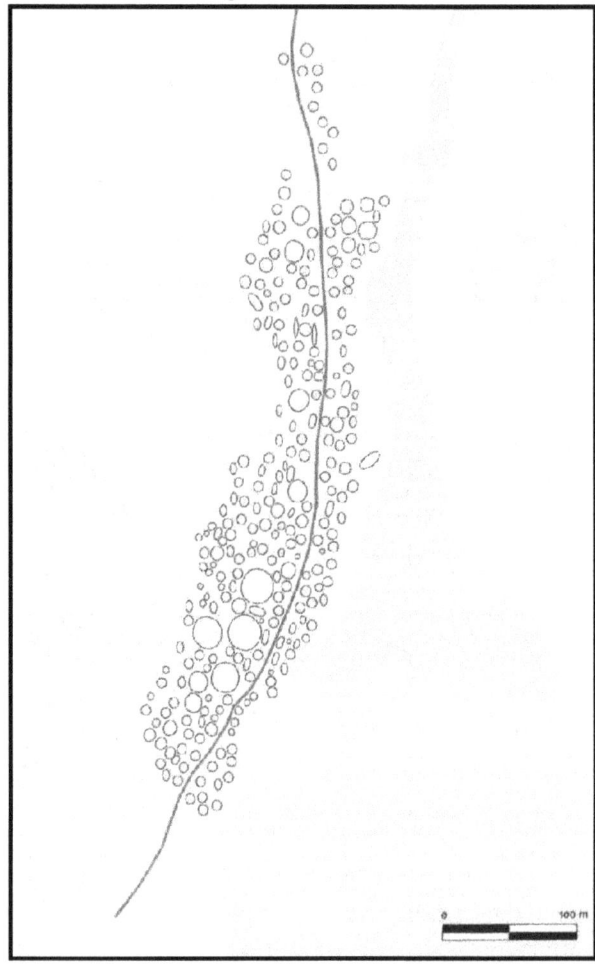

Figure 10. Map of the graves of Nordre Kaupang in relation to the probable route of the road (after Skre 2007b. Reproduced from Skre 2007, page 379. Copyright: The Kaupang Excavation Project.)

Chapter 5: The cemeteries at Kaupang

As a general note, none of the largest mounds on the site yielded finds. In fact, the richest graves at Nordre Kaupang are found in mid-sized to smallish mounds (Blindheim 1981a:73). The site has a mix of smaller and medium sized mounds, and long and round mounds are found in seeming confusion along the entire area, with no observable difference in wealth or positioning.

I will now take a look at the gender distribution on this cemetery. Out of 15 (archaeologically) sexed graves, six are female (one is a probable female grave) and nine are male (Blindheim 1981d:93; see Appendix for further details), if the southern tip of the cemetery is included. Earlier studies have described the barrows found towards the south of this strip of land as the southernmost tip of Nordre Kaupang cemetery, although Stylegar suggests we see this site as another cluster altogether, separate from Nordre Kaupang, and has called it Hagejordet (Stylegar2007:70). As the full geographical extent of any of the sites is no longer known, I believe it is difficult to determine this with any certainty. However, the graves positioning on the same strip of land as Nordre Kaupang, along with their exposition towards the fjord and not to the settlement, indicates to me that they can be seen as an extension of the Nordre Kaupang complex. Aside from the greater proximity to the settled area, these graves give the same impression as the majority of those from Nordre Kaupang: a detachment from the town, positioned at the foot of a hill, overlooking the fjord, but addressing themselves to the barrows of Nordre Kaupang rather than the town. If we include Hagejordet with the rest of Nordre Kaupang, we get a gender distribution as per the graph below:

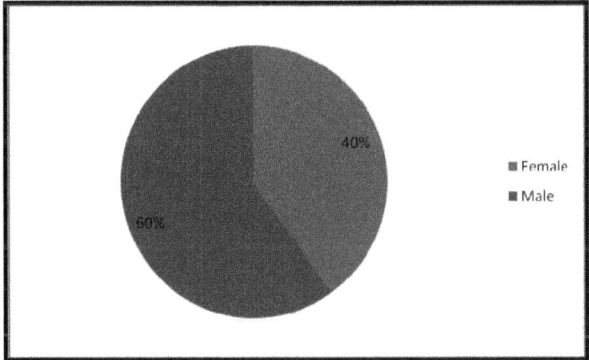

Figure 11. Male to female ratio of sexed graves at Nordre Kaupang (compiled with information from Lia 2001:appendix 5).

It is worth looking at a sample of the excavated female graves in a bit more detail. Nicolaysen's barrow 113 (Ka. 3), a female burial in a long barrow, whose finds included two oval brooches, along with some more unusual offerings such as an axe, and an iron rod, and a rattle, was interred in a long mound (Blindheim et al. 1981:200). The barrow lies at the western side of the cemetery down towards where an arm of the fjord jutted into the cemetery, and it is surrounded by round barrows several of which yielded no finds. The mound is aligned north-south, more or less in agreement with the alignment of the valley in which it lies. The overall impression given by the burial is that it is positioned towards the edges of the main burial site, but it does not stand alone and is not isolated.

Nicolaysen's barrow 85 (Ka. 10) is another female in a long barrow, found with oval brooches, beads, a spindle-whorl, but also with an axe, scythe, possible remnants of a horse bit, as well as remnants of an iron rod (Blindheim et al. 1981:204). Positioned on slightly higher ground than the previous example, this barrow is placed at the foot of the hills, seemingly aligned with the rising ground. Nicolaysen's barrows 77 and 94 are also long barrows, positioned near the middle of the site, one closer to the water, one closer to the hills. The last sexed female in the main part of the cemetery is found in barrow 60, located right in the middle of the cemetery, in close proximity to the large, though empty, round barrows. This is also a long barrow (Blindheim 1981d:94).

Nicolaysen's barrow 1 and 2 are found in the southern part of the strip of land which houses Nordre Kaupang (Stylegar 2007:70). These barrows were excavated by Blindheim's team during their investigations at Kaupang. The two barrows excavated (126 and 127) are both round, and they both yielded finds. One of them was sexed as female, the other one is uncertain (Stylegar 2007:72).

There is one noteworthy trait which characterises a large part of the female burial evidence: five out of the six sexed female graves are found in long, rather than round, mounds (Blindheim 1981d:93). The five definite female burials in the main area of Nordre Kaupang are all in long mounds and the female burial in a round mound is the one found at the southern tip of the site, somewhat removed from the main bulk of the burials (Stylegar 2007:72). There is no evidence of a male burial in a long mound at this site (Heyerdahl-Larsen 1981:57). From other sites at Kaupang, we know that women were buried in round mounds as well as long mounds, and it is curious there is no evidence of this from the main bulk of Nordre Kaupang. Are we perhaps dealing with a certain type of social role or function reserved for women, which afforded them the right to burial next to men, but which maintained the right, or perhaps need, to be set apart by outer markings? There are other long barrows which have yielded finds, but not of a type which can be used for decisive gendering, and so it cannot be concluded if they are male or female. However, based on the absence of weapons, and the complete lack of male burials in long barrows, it could be suggested that these are female. However, that is a rather bold suggestion which requires further in depth analysis before it can be asserted. As it is, I merely wish to point it out as a possibility at this stage.

Barrows containing female burials are dotted in amongst the male burials, and there seems no difference in the choice of positioning for them. They are equally visible, if not more so, because of their distinct shape. At this point, it is tempting to make conjectures about the meaning of the different outer marking, and much has been written on the potential symbolism of long mounds as resting places for women[11]. However, caution seems prudent, as many of the graves have remained unsexed, many were empty of finds, and a large number were never examined. I do not believe it can be conclusively said that all female burials at Nordre Kaupang were in long barrows, but we may be able to see a certain pattern of a distinct social role which gave the right to burial in different shaped mounds, and this point will be further discussed in the following chapter.

Returning to the argument that a traveller's way into, or out of Kaupang was meant to recall the legitimate power of those who belonged to the nearby farms and power centre (Skre:2007b), it becomes clear that both men and women formed a part of this power structure, and arguably were even meant to be seen to be part of it.

5.4 Lamøya

Another concentration of graves is found at Lamøya, at present on a peninsula, but which was an island in the Viking Age. Early written sources give no clear information about the extent of burials here, as the numbers vary greatly from one text to another. Only a few of the barrows at the site have been excavated. In 1902, Gustafson examined three barrows, one of which yielded two boat burials, both inhumations, one of which was gendered female and one male (Blindheim 1981c:85; Heyerdahl-Larsen 1995a:51). Blindheim's team also carried out some work at the site (Blindheim 1981c:85).

What is known for certain is that there are both burial mounds and flat graves known from the area (Heyerdahl-Larsen 1981:63). The flat graves are situated on Guristranda, a beach on the side of the island facing the town, and the barrows are dotted in between the hills, and from what we know contain inhumation burials. Based on the fact that the graves of Guristranda are adjacent to, but not intruding on each other, it is assumed they were somehow marked in the landscape in the time the cemetery was used (Heyerdahl-Larsen 1995b:93). At the present time, 94 barrows and three stone settings are known from Lamøya, although it has been conjectured that the site once held around 200 barrows (Stylegar 2007:74). Three of the known barrows are long barrows, the remaining are round (Stylegar 2007:74).

The barrows are found in clusters between the hills which shape the landscape, but it is hard to use this information to any purpose, due to the disturbance of agricultural activities and consequent loss of many barrows (Stylegar 2007:74). One of the common traits for the mounds on Lamøya is the curious topographical position, if considered in terms of visibility and dominance. If one is going to make the effort necessary to create a burial mound for someone, it might seem logical to place them somewhere they would be clearly visible, either in open terrain or on a slope perhaps. It entails a lot of effort, and the mere fact the grave is made into a mound, a visible marker, might indicate a wish to create a visual reminder of the departed. Not so with Lamøya's graves. A landscape dominated by hills and dips, the majority of Lamøya's mounds are found in the dips in between the hills[12]. The known barrows all have a view towards the fjord, but are closed off in other directions by the rising hills. Perhaps it can be said they command a view towards the fjord, or from the fjord. In fact, common for all the known graves at Lamøya is that they seem to be positioned in relation to the fjord with a view outwards to the water (Lia 2001:109). They will of course have been visible from the surrounding hills, but visibility from the barrows themselves would have been limited. There is a concentration of barrows towards the western shore of the site, facing Bikjholberget, which seem to be positioned in more open terrain. There are no apparent gender distinctions in terms of topographical positioning or wealth, and there is a distinct dominance of female graves in the excavated material. Out of six sexed burials, four are in fact female (see Appendix).

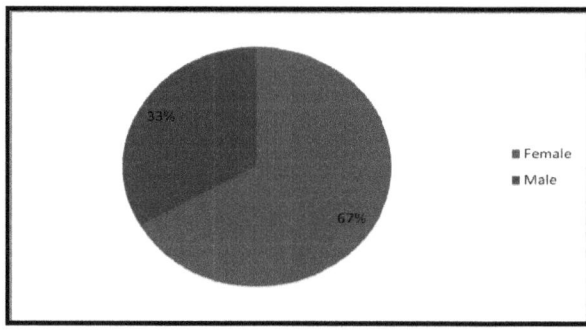

Figure 12. Male to female ratio of gendered graves at Lamøya (compiled with information from Lia 2001:appendix 5)

---

[11] Interpretations range from them being a substitute long hall for women, as this was the traditional domain of men, or symbols of ships to represent their status as widows of sea-faring men (see Tsigoridas 1998:2–3), to them being symbolic of female genitalia and linked to fertility cults (Tsigoridas 1998:12; Skogstrand 2002:455).

[12] It seems prudent to note the essential difference between the Lamøya graves and Oseberg, which was disussed in Chapter 4. Although Oseberg is also placed in between hills, it is in a much more open landscape, dominating a plain, The Lamøya graves are more tucked away in between the hills. Further, the number and the size of graves at Lamøya sets the site apart from the single monument of Oseberg.

Chapter 5: The cemeteries at Kaupang

One of the barrows they excavated by Blindheim's team was Ka. 218, or Dortehaugen (Heyerdahl-Larsen 1995a:51). This long barrow stood at 0,40 cm high, and was overgrown with vegetation at the time of excavation (Heyerdahl-Larsen 1995a:51). It was edged by a stone setting, and measured approximately 5,5 metres in width, with the outward shape being a long barrow. The human remains had been placed in a boat, and were accompanied by a selection of grave goods which has led to it being gendered female (Heyerdahl-Larsen 1995b:52). A flat grave excavated by the same team also gave a female grave with wealthy grave goods (Heyerdahl-Larsen 1995a:52). Of the burials excavated by Gustafson, one was an apparent double burial, male and female, in a barrow (Blindheim 1981b:85; Blindheim 1981e:109). Another two flat graves have been found, one male and one female (Blindheim et al. 1981:216).

The fact that the site was an island may give some clue to the symbolism of the landscape at Lamøya. Based on the fact that in order to cross water, one must use an external form of transport (or a mode of self transportation not as convenient as walking, i.e. swimming), I would argue that a body of water represents a stronger division than a body of land. Water is often ascribed importance in ritual meanings (Strang 2008:123), and it acts as a potent divider. Thus, the cemetery at Lamøya appears more strongly set apart from the settlement than the other burial sites, which are all reachable by land. This may point to that we are looking at a separate group of people buried here, distinguished or set apart for some reason. A few ideas on this will be discussed below.

As a result of Kaupang being a market place, and thus a place people travelled to, there have been conjectures that some of the burials may belong to travellers who passed away whilst staying in the town (Hofseth 1999:108). Physically removed from the mainland, reachable only by crossing water, it could be seen as logical that the graves destined for this site should have some connection with water. Following this train of thought, it could be said there may have been a connection with seaborne travel. The clearly defined separate position of these graves, the division drawn between them and the town by a boundary of water, may support an argument that these were graves that did not 'belong' to the town. A body of water may have acted as a strong dividing line between the living and the dead (Lund 2009:219). Are we perhaps looking at the graves of 'foreign' merchants and traders? It seems not unlikely that Kaupang would have had a constant contingent of non-native settlers, who had come there to work or trade. Not fully assimilated into the local culture, it may be that on the event of their death, they were given a visibly distinct burial – the same in terms of outward shape and ritual perhaps, as of those who belonged to the area, but distinct nonetheless for being separated from the mainland. Speaking against this theory however is the fact that there are no distinct traits observed in the actual grave goods, no particular evidence of imports or foreign artefacts (Heyerdahl-Larsen 1995a:51-52), and we cannot safely do more than speculate on why these graves were placed in a separate body of land to the other cemeteries.

Another way of interpreting the positioning of the site on an island which speaks against the above interpretation is that can be seen as a barrier between travellers and the town, the first thing that would greet an arrival by the sea route. A traveller would need to pass by this cemetery, where so many of the graves were clearly visible from the sea, and thus the argument might be taken in the opposite direction – that these people did indeed belong to the town, and perhaps served a similar purpose as the Nordre Kaupang graves, of demonstrating continuity and legitimacy through ancestors, deliberately displayed to arriving or departing travellers.

However it may be, the cemetery remains marked as a separate entity which one would need to cross water in order to get to, and in order to carry out burial rituals physical transportation across water would be required. What reason there was for this separate location can only be guessed at until more is known of the graves at the site. As so few of the barrows have been excavated, I do not feel much can be said in terms of gender division,
except that women as well as men were represented here, both in flat graves and barrows.

5.5 Bikjholberget

Bikjholberget is the last of the larger concentration of graves currently known in the area, and provides an interesting contrast to the cremation graves in barrows prevalent at Nordre Kaupang. Bikjholberget is dominated by flat graves, with inhumations as the prevailing custom. Excavated by Blindheim's team in the 1950s, the site was dealt with during excavation in terms of a northern and a southern part, but is seen as one large site. The northern part of the site is completely flat, and has seen a lot of disturbance through different domestic activities (Blindheim 1995b:55). The southern part however, has a large number of intact graves, often rich in grave goods. Many of the graves here are marked by stone settings, and there is a distinct dominance of boat burials, although there are also burials in coffins and chamber graves, as well as graves with no visible internal markings (Heyerdahl-Larsen 1995b:92). It is assumed that a large part of the site remains unexcavated, and so the full extent of cemetery is to date unknown (Stylegar 2007:73).

The cemetery is positioned on a hill, which forms a clear visual feature in the landscape. In the Viking Age the hill would have jutted into the fjord, making it even more conspicuous, and it could be clearly seen from the town, being located a mere 150 metres away from it. The site commands a view over its surroundings, both sea and land, in contrast with the other burial sites at Kaupang, which bear aspects of being more sheltered and less exposed towards their surroundings. I will take a brief look at one of the more complex graves found, in order to give some impression of the type of evidence which has been found at this site:

Ka. 294 – 297 (Grave K/IV) is one of the decidedly more complex graves of the site. It contains a boat burial, covered with a setting of stones. Positioned near the foot of a hill, and aligned north/south (Heyerdahl-Larsen 1995a:22), it contained a total of four individuals, two of whom were male, and two female, with a female burial in either end of the boat, one male in the middle, and one male under the boat (Heyerdahl-Larsen 1995a:23; Stylegar 2007:95). The woman placed in the south of the boat was buried with two oval brooches, as well as a trefoil brooch. She also had a silver ring, and beads, as well as a key, knife and weaving sword, an arrowhead and an axe (Heyerdahl-Larsen 1995a:23-24; Stylegar 2007:95). It is possible she had an infant placed in the grave with her (Stylegar 2007:95). The man in the middle of the boat was accompanied by a horse, a sword, arrowheads and remnants of shields. The woman positioned in the north of the boat was found with remnants of oval brooches, the remains of a dog, a hanging bowl, riding equipment, and what was believed to be a meat roasting spit, but which more recent research has suggested may be interpreted as the staff of a volve (Heyerdahl-Larsen 1995a:24; Stylegar 2007:95). The male burial found under the boat was accompanied by weapons in the shape of spearhead and knives, a penannular brooch, and other small items such as a strike-alight and a hone (Stylegar 2007:123). This burial is dated to the 9th century, whilst the three in the boat are given a date of early 10th century (Stylegar 2007:95). The position of this grave, near to the foot of a hill, indicates a liminal position, approaching the edges of the area. The contents also lend themselves easily to an interpretation in a ritual context, as will be discussed in more detail in the following chapter.

The presence of four individuals in this grave, three of which were in the actual boat, makes the interpretation difficult, although I believe there is enough evidence to make a ritual explanation defensible. Are we faced with members of the same prominent family, of which one member had ritual power? Were they all connected with cult and ritual? At the very least, it seems logical to conclude that individuals buried in the same grave were in some way connected to each other. I believe the idea of human sacrifices can be ruled out on the basis that they were all afforded individual grave goods. Also, the fact it contains both genders seems to testify towards an equal standing in society, though perhaps reinforced by one woman's ritual connections. The two female burials are particularly lavish, but the male ones are in no way poor. The male burial below the boat raises questions in connection with his singular positioning, but an explanation may be sought in the earlier dating of this burial – perhaps the later burials shared a connection with him, through family or social identities.

Of the other female graves at Bikjholberget, there are others with ritual links, but this does not appear to be a prerequisite. The female burials are found intermixed with male interments in terms of location, often in the same grave. Again, there are more sexed male burials than there are female, but this appears to be the only distinguishing trait in terms of distribution. Out of 56 sexed graves, 36 are male and 20 female (see Appendix). Due to the poor preservation conditions for skeletal remains, the majority of the graves have been archaeologically gendered rather than osteologically sexed (Blindheim and Heyerdahl-Larsen 1995b:116).

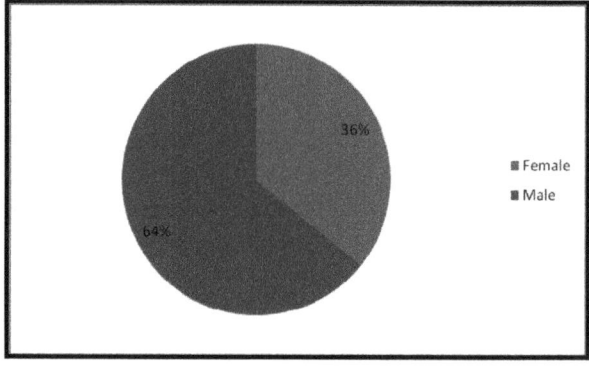

Figure 13. Male to female ratio at Bikjholberget (compiled with information from Lia 2001:appendix5).

Øystein Lia pointed to the high ritual context of Bikjholberget, where some graves show traces of violence in the form of dismemberment, or axes hewn into the graves as well as high numbers of animal sacrifices, along with artefacts often interpreted in ritual contexts, such as rattles (Lia 2002:302). The act of embedding a weapon, such as an axe or a spear, into a completed burial is not unheard of from the surrounding areas, and may be interpreted as part of the burial rites (Lund 2009:66). One potential link can be found in stories of spears being thrown over an enemy army in battle, to 'mark them for Odin', meaning that those who go to Odin after death are marked with a spear (Price 2002:139). Interestingly, many of the site's numerous boat burials also have stone settings, which creates a paradox if the boat is interpreted as a means of travel to the realms of the dead, and the stone setting as a means of keeping the dead securely in the grave. One may perhaps be justified in drawing a parallel to the seaworthy ship of Oseberg, securely anchored inside its mound.

So far then this very brief description Bikjholberget has given us little clue as to the topographical significance of positioning of graves. It may be suggested that the

Chapter 5: The cemeteries at Kaupang

more liminal graves placed near the foot of the hill had some ritual connection, but both genders are buried in all sections of the cemetery, and as was pointed out by Blindheim and Heyerdahl-Larsen, there is in fact nothing at this site which indicates that women were discriminated against (Heyerdahl-Larsen 1995b:125). Due to the lack of individual visibility in the landscape of the flat graves, I believe this site is best treated as a whole, rather than in terms of individual graves. There is evidence of graves intruding on each other, and disturbing earlier contexts (Blindheim and Heyerdal-Larsen 1995a:113), which suggests the possibility they were not always clearly marked in the time when the site was in use. It could also indicate a lack of space, resulting in removal and reburial (Blindheim and Heyerdahl-Larsen 1995a:113). At the same time, the graves at this site are by no means lacking in grave goods, and many are wealthy (Blindheim and Heyerdahl-Larsen 1995 b:125). It seems it was enough to be buried on this hill, and that further concerns of positioning were not credited much importance. Perhaps just being buried at this site was prestige enough, and that no further need for distinction by outwards shape of the burial was needed? There is of course a certain similarity between barrows and hills such as this, and perhaps its natural shape may have been a contributing factor when this specific spot was chosen as a cemetery. In this case, the question becomes what was needed in order to given the privilege of being buried here. My belief is social visibility and active social status, and judging from the mixed male and female burials present and their intermixed positioning, I will put forward the suggestion that this was attainable to both male and female social actors. Bikjholberget, aside from its ritual links, also has quite a few burials which show some gender ambiguity. There are female graves with weapons (aside from axes, which are relatively common in women's graves, there are also incidents of arrowheads and spear points), and there are male graves with typical female goods such as textile production tools (Lia 2002:306). This implies a greater degree of gender mobility than what is often assigned to the Late Iron Age in Norway. Further, judging from the positioning of the site, open to view from the town, and from the approach into it, both by land and sea, as well as the fact that the town was clearly visible from the site, I believe it reasonable to tie the status of the buried individuals directly to the town, and to suggest that we may be looking at the graves of the town dignitaries, and more prominent social players. The boats and the relative wealth of imported goods (Lia 2001:9) point to association with travel, but in a busy port town, this might be a natural link for any person of distinction – either through direct engagement in trade, or through ties with such activities.

5.6 Conclusion

As we have seen then, the mortuary landscape of the Kaupang area is varied: in location, outer shape of the graves, inner structure and body treatment. It seems clear that we are dealing with a highly complex culture, where different concerns and traditions made themselves apparent in the treatment of the dead (Blindheim 1981c:91), such as might perhaps be expected from a town where different influences made themselves known through travel and links with the outside world. In summary, the following points can be made:

- The largest of the cemeteries, Nordre Kaupang is made up of barrows and cremations (Heyerdahl-Larsen 1981; Lia 2001). This site has a relatively high number of female burials, with no visible difference in the positioning of graves. However, there is a distinguishing trait in that the vast majority of sexed female graves that are found in long, rather than round mounds (Heyerdahl-Larsen 1981:57). The cemetery shows evidence of a different topographical positioning from other sites, in that it does not directly communicate with the town, and Skre's suggestion of it being the resting place of the wealthy landowners of the surrounding area seems likely (Skre 2007b).

- Lamøya holds both barrow graves and flat graves, but few have been excavated. From the excavated material, there are a majority of gendered female graves. The cemetery forms a clearly visible feature both from the town, and for travellers arriving by sea, but the dividing line of water between the graves and the town raises questions about the beliefs behind such a positioning.

- Bikjholberget's positioning on a hill, clearly visible in the landscape has led to the suggestion of its role as a burial place for people of status and importance. The high number of female burials (Blindheim and Heyerdahl-Larsen 1995b:125) here allows us to make the suggestion that women were part of this upper social tier, and that they were credited importance as individual players.

- Of the different burial rites, there appears no discernable distinction in wealth between flat graves or barrows, inhumations or cremations (Blindheim 1981d:119), and the different cemeteries appear to have been used simultaneously (Blindheim 1995a:13).

On this premise, I will now turn to a discussion of the evidence which has been presented so far, in which I will attempt to drawn on both the Oseberg case and the site of Kaupang.

Chapter 6. Discussion

The aim of this chapter will be to pull together the evidence discussed in the previous chapters, in order to see if any general conclusions can be drawn from what has been presented. Specifically, the focus will be on individual social visibility, and any apparent gender differences visible in the landscape.

6.1 Summary of findings

Before proceeding to the main discussions, a summary of the key points presented seems appropriate:

- Burial mounds of a monumental size were used as a status symbol attainable to both men and women, although excavated examples show higher numbers of male burials.

- In terms of positioning, outer shape and wealth of grave goods, there are no discernable gender based differences which can be observed as a universal rule. This suggests that the ideology behind the burials was the same for either gender, as the similarity in shape and positioning suggests the symbolic coding would have been the same.

- Traditional interpretations of the Oseberg burial has tended to remove it from the public sphere, in which other monumental graves are firmly placed. In Chapter 4, I set out the reasons why I believe this is not necessarily appropriate, and I will proceed to discuss some implications of traditional interpretations and the possibilities of new lines of enquiry.

- The Kaupang area shows a proliferation of different burial rites in terms of internal treatment, external markers and positioning, as has been summarised in Chapter 5. However, a common trait for the Kaupang cemeteries is that they all give evidence of female burials, buried alongside their male contemporaries, with no apparent difference in wealth or positioning. Again, the only discernable difference is in the numbers, which show a decided bias towards a predominance of male burials on at least two of the main sites (Nordre Kaupang and Bikjholberget). Outer shape is also often the same, apart from in the case of Nordre Kaupang, where a substantial number of the female graves are found in long burial mounds rather than round.

In summary, traits such as visibility and conspicuousness in the landscape appears to have been considered in equal measure for monuments raised over male or female individuals.

This chapter will aim to answer some questions which arise from the above points, in terms of social standing, social fluidity, status markers, and archaeological methods. I will start with asking the most obvious question: is the marginalised role of women which we so often encounter in representations of Viking Age society a true representation of the evidence at hand, or is it tainted by assumptions based on more modern values? It is my suggestion that our understanding is influenced by the discipline's Victorian roots in combination with a reliance on written sources dating largely from medieval times.

6.2 Women on the margins: of Viking Age social order or archaeological interpretation?

As we have seen, the most spectacular grave known from Viking Age Norway, the Oseberg mound, housed the remains of two women (Christensen et al. 1993:7). As is only too common in cases where we deal with the graves of women of wealth, interpretations have tended to push these women out of the public sphere, and away from an active political role (Pedersen 2008:586). Such women will become at best the wife or mother of a ruler, always the consort, never the ruling power (Pedersen 2008:586). There is a distinct observable bias towards associating powerful women with men in order to make sense of them, and Oseberg has not been exempted from this. The Oseberg 'queen' has been the mother of a Viking after Brøgger's Åsa theory (Brøgger 1916), a sacrificial victim (Gansum 1995), or at best a priestess and ruler, but always something of an anomaly in the male-oriented power landscape (Ingstad 1995), as seems manifested by the Åsa theory which ties the 'queen' to written sources and identifies her as one of the few women mentioned at length in the Yngliga Saga (Pedersen 2008:588; Sturlason 1943). When Gansum remarks it is a point to be considered that the Oseberg mound is not mentioned in textual sources such as Snorre, and uses this to back up his argument of the mound as a religious sacrifice, outside the arena of power (Gansum 1995:134), this betrays in my opinion a heavy reliance on textual sources which disregards actual archaeological evidence. This exemplifies a trend which I believe must be abandoned if we are to gain a balanced and unbiased view of Viking Age gender relations. If evidence in the landscape shows that men and women were buried in closely comparable sites and ways, this may indicate that the belief in the Vikings as 'irredeemably male' (Jesch 1994:1) may need to be reconsidered. The archaeological landscape has been shaped by both men and women, whereas the textual evidence which relates to the Viking Age has been written by men (Gräslund 2001:81), a point which ought to be considered if either of these sources are to be given primacy.

Chapter 6: Discussion

Similarly to Oseberg, Kaupang is often pointed out as being outside the norm in relation to the high number of gendered female graves present. As we have seen, the marked variation between the different burial customs at Kaupang, point to a difference in beliefs or at least in burial rituals within the society belonging to the area (Blindheim 1981c:91), but these divisions do not appear to be gender based. It can be concluded that there are at least three distinct cemeteries at Kaupang, perhaps serving different purposes. The barrow cemetery of Nordre Kaupang may be conjectured to have served the authority of the nearby landowners (after Skre's suggestion 2007b). Bikjholberget, based on its clear visual communication with the township, may arguably be the cemetery with the closest ties to the town, reserved for those individuals and perhaps families who held prominent positions in the local town community. Lamøya appears to represent something different with its combination of flat graves and barrows placed on an island. The common denominator for these sites however, is that they all show variety in grave goods, which indicate the presence of different social functions and different genders.

It is my belief that these two sites (Oseberg, standing as it does at the top of the social pyramid in terms of status symbols and wealth, and Kaupang, a site known for its urban nature, reflecting a wide spectrum of social functions and roles), testify to a rather more integrated role for female social players than what is often allowed for in archaeological interpretations. As I have attempted to make clear throughout this study, I do not wish to challenge the idea that the people of the Viking Age knew gender as an important structuring category. I also fully accept that there were differences in terms of gender ideology[13], of what was the norm to which either gender ought to conform[14]. However, what I propose is that we move away from relying on stereotypes when we look for social structures in the past, and towards an approach which relies on archaeological evidence, in this case specifically, on mortuary evidence in the landscape. I will proceed to explain the basis for my arguments in more detail below.

For argument's sake, we will now turn briefly to the idea that in a society based on trade and commerce, such as is seen at Kaupang, there may be more potential for social mobility than in a traditional rural society (see for example Hofseth 1999 for this type or argument), it seems probable there were a higher number of social roles and occupations between which to choose, which in turn may have led to greater social flexibility. This in turn may be seen to account for the high numbers of female graves at Kaupang, as well as the fact that they are never separate from their male counterparts in terms of positioning, or behind them in wealth. The fallacy of this argument however, lies in narrowing down the role of social agency, and the scope for diverging into specialised roles in settings other than the purely urban. This tends to close off the importance of individual ambition and action to the majority of the population, and I believe this kind of limitation for the sake of creating a valid argument (here, the upwards transgression of women normally assumed to be less socially visible than men made possibly by a strict set of circumstances) does as much damage as good. It reinforces the message of active males / passive females, by setting a firm, archaeological example of active females aside as a possibility, but as an anomaly.

Rather than asking 'why are there so many women found here?' we could ask 'why are there so few women found elsewhere?' The latter question could then be used to examine differences in excavation technique, sampling, gendering of the remains and gender markers. I believe a lot can be gained from looking further into arguments such as the one presented by Stylegar, where he attributes the fall in female graves in the 10th century at Kaupang to a change of female costume, rather than a sudden fall in their social standing (Stylegar 2007:83). If this argument is taken a little further, it can also be suggested that in an urban society, fashion accessories such as brooches may have been more readily available than in a rural setting where the trade and productions links may not be so pronounced. It must remain a possibility that our 'lack' of female graves can be attributed, at least in part, to excavation methods, and prevalent methods of gendering remains. If this is admitted as a possibility, the evidence must also be further examined in order to either be admitted as feasible, or to be ruled out. One approach to re-examining this is, as I hope this study has demonstrated, through the landscape and relative positioning of mortuary monuments.

6.3 Power and influence, the different faces of status

Dommasnes in her 1998 article on gender and power in the Norwegian Iron Age, brought attention to the different aspects of openly acknowledged power, and the more subtle form of influence, where she argued that the latter belonged to women through their role in the household (Dommasnes 1998), and this type of questioning remains complex and interesting. I feel however that this argument may rely too heavily on modern day value assignments, as I will attempt to show below through discussing the legitimacy of transferring our own ideas of significance and status to the past.

---

[13] Gender ideology is here understood as the 'meanings and values attributed to gender categories in a given culture' (after Hays-Gilpin, K., and Whitley, D., (eds) 1998:xv)

[14] I also work, as stated earlier in this paper, on the assumption that the late Iron Age in Norway knew two genders as the norm. Exceptions might occur, but from what we know from written evidence as well as archaeoligcal evidence, there seems to have been a clear assignment of values to male and female.

One important aspect relating to the archaeology of power is how much of our own structures we can and ought to transfer on the past, and assume as 'natural'. From a gender perspective, this means asking if we should be measuring power in terms of male standards, and trying to fit women into a male norm (Hjørungdal 1991:64). Anyone interested in women's roles in the Late Iron Age Norway will have read time and again about how women's roles were 'innanstokks', meaning indoors, anchored in the house. Countless sources accept this model, because after all, our written sources tell us it is so (Dommasnes 1998:338; Høgestøl 1985:56; Stalsberg 2001:75). I have two fundamental questions concerning this:

Can archaeologists rely on written sources that are not considered accurate historical or ethnographical sources (Lund 2009:24), and which we know were written down in a culture different from that which we are studying?

Assuming that the woman's place was indeed in the house, is it sound archaeology to assume that this means she was a less valued, less visible and less influential member of society than most men? Presumably, the women who ruled the household also ruled supplies and resources, and thus by extension the wealth of the household (Kristoffersen 1999b:294). Can we then say it is likely that these individuals were not considered powerful, and thus dismiss their social importance? Or should we perhaps explore the possibility that what is now considered private had more public importance in the Late Iron Age (Gräslund 2001:83)?

These questions will be examined in more detail below.

6.4 Female power: witches, shield maidens and matrons?

Textual sources have testified to that certain religious roles were associated with women, such as being a volve, a woman of religious power (Price 2002:73). An interesting line of inquiry could be followed from the fact that artefacts with ritual associations have been found in several female graves at Nordre Kaupang and Bikjholberget (roasting spits, alternatively interpreted as or volve staffs and a rattle to name some, see Appendix for further detail), but there are some difficulties with this argument. This is not least because there is also evidence of ritual artefacts found in male graves (Lia 2001:56). We will look a bit further into this line of enquiry here:

The so called meat roasting spits which are found in several female graves throughout Scandinavia are somewhat ambiguous. They are finds in a class of their own, the idea of them being cooking implements presumably having sprung from the association of women with hearth and home when in fact they are a very awkward shape for such an implement (Price 2002:189). The alternative interpretation of them as volve staffs is given strength by appearance of these utensils in graves with other ritual accoutrements, and the description of volvur as staff bearers (Price 2002:127–175). The staff is also referred to in certain written sources in terms which associate it with heathen practices: 'no man shall have in his house staff or altar, device for sorcery or sacrificial offering, or whatever relates to heathen practice' (as stated in the Eidsivating law, from Price 2002:175). I believe this argument is a realistic interpretation, and the idea also seems to have been accepted by other archaeologists, as for example Stylegar (2007:96).

The argument raised for Oseberg earlier in this study in terms of the possibility that women may have used ritual associations to increase their influence, may perhaps be of value here, but there is a certain danger in entering into this sort of argument. It can too easily push women into a 'hidden' ritual role, depriving them of potential visibility in interpretations, by moving them from what is considered to be the public sphere of action and affording them power only in a closed, cultic environment (See Gansum 1995; Ingstad 1995:147).

Figure 14. Possible Volve staff? (reproduced with the permission of the Oslo Kulturhistorisk museum, University of Oslo © Kulturhistorisk museum, Universitetet i Oslo)

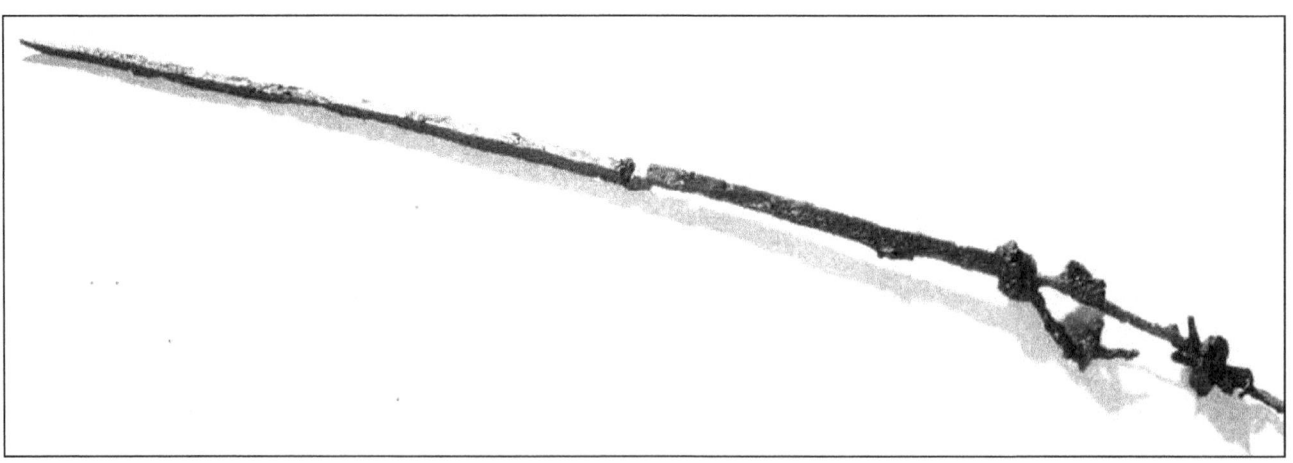

Chapter 6: Discussion

The issue here is of course not with religious roles being hidden, it is related to modern interpretations which tend dismiss the cultic sphere as being outside the normal area of political power (see for example Gansum 1997:38; Pedersen 2008:587). However, as written evidence exists of this class of woman, it may provide an easy avenue of interpretations in the case of women who appear independent and wealthy (Price 2002:113).

There are descriptions of the professional, travelling volve from sagas and other sources, who was paid for her services of making prophecies and who commanded respect, and sometimes fear, in the community (Price 2002:113). The art of seið gave power to those who had knowledge of it: according to Snorre, Odin had knowledge of this art which brought the 'greatest power' (Solli 1999:400). But this channel of power was mainly reserved for women, and was considered a shameful activity for men (Solli 1999:400). As discussed earlier, there are artefacts in the Oseberg find which can point to cultic significance. Aside from the two staffs discussed in chapter four, there are the tapestries, which have often been interpreted as depicting ritual processions and proceedings (Ingstad 1993b:234; Ingstad 1995:142). Also of potential importance is the richly decorated wagon, which belongs to a category of grave goods commonly found with wealthy female burials in Scandinavia (Price 2002:139). Wagons can be linked with Freyja, who was known to travel in a wagon pulled by cats, and who was the original god of seiðr (Price 2002:160; Steinsland 1994a:149). The Oseberg wagon also carries a design of cats on one of the carved sides (Ingstad 1993b:250; Price 2002:160). The link of cats with volvur is further cemented by the description given of a volve in Eirik Raudes Saga, which talks of her wearing gloves of cat-skin (Hedeager 1999:74–75). There are also arguments for linking textile work, especially weaving, to ritual activities, sources tell us of women weaving fortunes (Heide 2006:236–260; Synnestvedt 2002:139), and of the Nornir, the spinning goddesses of fate (Jochens 1996:39). As mentioned in Chapter 4, there was a quantity of textile working tools found in the Oseberg burial. I consider it likely that women might tap into ritual power to cement and thus increase influence and power, but this ought not become a template for all women of higher status. There are several examples of women found with artefacts which lend themselves easily to a ritual interpretation (Price 2002:127), but this is far from being a general rule. Individual agency is what must be stressed here – I suggest it was a path to power and influence, but not the only one available for women.

Another aspect of interest are the medieval descriptions of 'shield maidens', such as is found in Hervorar Saga ok Heiðreks (Lund 2009:252–253). In this tale, Hervor the shield maiden wakes her dead father in his burial mound and demands he passes on her sword to her, with which he was buried. This he does, and she goes on to use the sword in battle (Lund 2009:253-253). It has been commonly assumed that the idea of the Viking warrior woman was a product of the Middle Ages (Jochens 1996 in Price 2002:111), and it has been described with some disdain as the imaginings of the men who wrote the sagas (Price 2002:111). Indeed, there is no archaeological evidence to suggest women were buried with weapons on the same scale as men. There are of course exceptions, as we will return to later in this chapter, but this cannot lend strength to an argument of women in the warrior group as the norm. It can rather be seen to raise interesting questions around social fluidity.

An interesting aspect of the warrior women stories is found when examining the testimony of written sources. An Arabian diplomat traveller during the 10th century to parts of Europe, Ibn Fadlan was the author of ethnographic accounts of what he saw amongst those people he encountered (Warmind 1995:131). The writings of Ibn Fadlan are often accepted as a trustworthy source on aspects of burial ritual (Lia 2002:312; Price 2002:221; Warmind 1995:131–135), such as for the practice of human sacrifice, for which there actually is very little archaeological evidence. At the same time, we have a written source in the form of the writings of Cedrenus, which speaks of fighting women, but which is a rarely mentioned source (Price 2002:332). Dating from 970, this account details an attack by the Rus against the Byzantines, in the aftermath of which the Byzantines were recorded as being surprised by the number of women they found amongst the dead on the battlefield (Price 2002:332). There is also mention of warrior women in Saxo's History of the Danes (Jesch 1994:176). On the one hand then, one account of customs of the Rus is accepted as a viable source, and another is all but forgotten. In my opinion, the acceptance of the 'eye – witness' account of Ibn Fadlan as reliable is not without its problems: there is the fact that Ibn Fadlan did not speak or understand the language of the people he observed, but relied on an interpreter, as well as clear signs in his account that he relied on interpreting what he saw into a ritual 'language' he could understand (Warmind 1995:132). His descriptions of paradise as 'green and beautiful' for instance, seems more applicable to his own faith over that associated with the Viking Age beliefs, where we have no knowledge of such a world for the afterlife (Sass 1995:136–138; Warmind 1995:134). I do not believe we can put much faith in the 'ethnography' of Ibn Fadlan as a true historical account, although if used with caution, I believe the text can be used to offer interpretations of archaeological finds. This being said, if we do let Ibn Fadlan on the scene as a serviceable source, surely we must consider treating other, contemporary sources with equal respect?

Returning to the possibility of gender fluidity in the warrior role, the female Valkyrie deserves some attention. They are rather gruesome and violent creatures, the 'choosers of the slain' who pick out the warriors determined for Odin's Valhalla (Price 2002:331–336). Price has highlighted the description in the Darraðljóð text, which shows a scene where women determine the fate of battle by weaving on a loom with men's intestines for thread and human heads for weights (Price 2002: 395). There is an aspect of female involvement in battle and violence seen through the Valkyrie and their potential to decide men's fates, as well as in the hints towards sorcery as a weapon of war (Price 2002: 395). The point here is not to suggest women fought alongside men on as a rule, but to suggest that we ought perhaps to open up alternative avenues of interpretation which allow for other types of involvement in battle other than the traditional male, warrior role. It is also worth mentioning that the goddess Freyja had strong links with battle and war – as a hostess to dead warriors and a chooser of the slain, she was a goddess of war as well as fertility (Price 2002:108).

Moving on to the questions around what was public and what was private in the Iron Age, we must look at the type of social organisation which was prevalent. Evidence points to large farms as the core of social structure, acting as both cultic and administration centres (Kristoffersen 2004b:61; Skre 2007a:19). The performance of religious or cultic acts was 'privatized' in that it was carried out by the lady of the house and her husband on large farms (Fuglestvedt 1997:44). I stated earlier that keys were a female power symbol: medieval laws described how in marriage a woman is presented with the keys of the household, which represents the wealth of the farm. Siv Kristoffersen has in her work examined keys and textile tools as accoutrements of power for women of a certain social group in the Migration period in Norway. This group is termed 'Lady of the House', and is made up of women who were in charge of the distribution of wealth, as well as important production processes such as textile production (Kristoffersen 1999a; Kristoffersen 1999b; Kristoffersen 2002; Kristoffersen 2004a; Kristoffersen 2004b). In this type of role, it becomes apparent that the rule of the wealth of the farm is more than a mere private control of household economy. The role bears little relation to the ideal of the housewife imposed on women in the last couple of centuries, and cannot be believed to have represented a limitation of power, but rather an expression thereof. These farms served as administrative centres, and whoever held a role of power there did not belong to the 'private' sphere (Kristoffersen 2004b:61). Thus, the association of women with the home becomes something different than what is has come to mean in contemporary western society, and represents rather an avenue for power than a hidden role. The material examined by Kristoffersen belongs to an earlier period than what has been discussed in this study, but it is often assumed that there was a certain continuity in social aspects such as gender roles and ritual beliefs throughout the Norwegian Iron Age (see for example Dommasnes 1998). This leads to the possibility that the assumed 'private' of the farmstead in the Viking Age may have been a far more public arena than what has often been assumed. We may need to move towards a more nuanced picture of the past, and accept that cultural aspects of power in the past may not be classifiable by sharp binary oppositions which correspond with current prevalent ideals.

6.5 Kaupang and Oseberg – exceptional or representative of a wider trend?

Oseberg contains the graves of two women, of exceptional wealth and grandeur. Had this been the grave of a man, it would perhaps be labelled the grave of a local chieftain, such as Gokstad has been, and no more questions would have been asked about the identity of the individuals, at least not beyond a typical attempt to link an historic king from the Ynglinga stories to the grave. For Oseberg however, archaeologists have been seeking alternative explanations for nearly a century. Interpretations will often state that the Oseberg burial must have contained a queen, and will even go so far as to say that it would be meaningless to assume anything else. The justification for this is that there are no other female graves of comparable wealth known (Ingstad 1993b:229 –230). This to my mind exemplifies the problem I have tried to highlight in my study. If something appears unprecedented, need that automatically mean it is to be brushed aside as an anomaly? Or should we turn towards widening our understanding on the basis of finds which go against the accepted norms which have been assigned to the Viking Age? Another objection raised to seeing Oseberg as a political manifestation has been that female chieftains do not appear in written sources (Pedersen 2008:587). As will already have been made clear in this study, I do not believe that written sources can be given primacy over archaeological ones. When archaeological evidence points to high status and social visibility for some women, it seems poor archaeology to discount this in favour of written accounts.

I wish to bring attention to the question raised by Pedersen: is it really too radical to suggest that we admit the women of Oseberg into the higher tiers of social power, not as anomalies or as exceptions to the rule of men, but as independent social players, capable of forming their own destinies and attaining power enough to grant a burial such as was erected only for the elite, the chosen few who had ruled well and earned a lasting tribute to their memory (Pedersen 2008:590)? If the chieftain of Gokstad was buried in a manifestation of his secure power rather than needing the dominance of the Borre graves (Gansum 1995:223), then I believe that Oseberg reflects a similar situation. Or indeed we can turn this on its head, and say that Gokstad may need to be interpreted in a ritual light. The important issue is that one monument ought not be treated differently purely on the grounds of the gender of those buried within it, as appears to often be the case with Oseberg, when in fact we are looking at

Chapter 6: Discussion

such similar topographical situations as to make no possible case for differentiation on the basis of location. Another interesting issue here is the presence of female markers, such as a spindle-whorl in the ship barrow' at Borre (Gansum and Myhre 2003:68), which begs the question if the male power symbol of the ship-barrow at Borre can in fact be securely gendered as male. Without entering into a further discussion on this, it can also be mentioned that the barrow which covered the Borre ship was a long barrow, not round as was the more common shape (Sjøvold 1971:74). I have already remarked on the connection of long mounds with female graves (Tsigaridas 1998:2), and will not go much further with this, other than leaving it as an interesting point for thought. Brøgger wrote that Borre was most likely a man's burial, even though it lacked any strong male markers (Brøgger 1916:19), but there is no evidence to support this supposition. The only basis for this argument, is that as the burial displays no definite female markers, it must be male (Brøgger 1916:19). The weakness of this argument hardly needs elaborating on. Myhre and Gansum have gone so far as to suggest both a male and a female might have been buried there, or that the (male) ship barrow covered an earlier (female) burial (Myhre and Gansum 2003:68 – 69), but there is no persuasive evidence for this theory either. I believe the evidence shows we must admit this as an uncertain burial, which could be either male or female.

The fact that the Oseberg women were women should not need to be explained. It ought to be accepted, to provoke further study of the gender roles of the Vikings and our understanding of these, rather than generate attempts to fit it into a preconceived gender structure, as previous studies tend to do. Surely, archaeology ought to use the material evidence found to challenge preconceived ideas and values transferred on to the past, rather than try and explain away evidence which goes against accepted theories, which savours strongly of fitting evidence into existing theories.

Kaupang represents an altogether different burial tradition. The graves are still affluent, but nowhere near approaching Oseberg's wealth. They are usually marked in the landscape, but as part of a cemetery, not as lone standing monuments. However, there is good evidence of different gender markers in these social strata as well. All the cemeteries have given evidence of both male and female graves and there is very little which distinguish the graves of men from women. There is a noticeably higher number of male graves than female, but it is in fact hard to know if this is due to the vagaries of excavation, the fact that traditional female 'markers' in terms of grave goods are smaller or made of perishable materials (Blindheim and Heyerdahl-Larsen 1995b:126), and more easily missed than male burials, or if it really was the case that more men were buried in a distinctly visible way than women due to their higher status. From an early age in archaeology, there has been a certain concern that stray finds are more easily noticed and recorded if they are of a larger nature, such as weapons (Pettersen 1928 in Forseth 1993:76). A stray oval brooch may easily be passed by or overlooked (Sjøvold 1944:82), this may also help account for the imbalance in gendered male and female finds. Along the same lines of enquiry is the question of whether typical female grave goods may have been of a more perishable nature, and whether large metal objects such as swords may have more easily survived (Sjøvold 1944:82). It has been remarked that the ratio of male to female graves is more equal in sites which have been professionally excavated (Løken 1974:69), as manifested by the high number of female graves at Kaupang. This may explain the lack of female graves in certain contexts. Changes in customs of dress and adornment must also be allowed for. It may be argued therefore, that the heavy bias towards male graves is more a result of archaeological methods and priorities than of actual social conditions in the past. It certainly ought not come as a surprise that women could and at times did hold an active role in social settings. I also believe we must avoid the temptation of assigning a special status to Kaupang in terms of gender equality on the basis of its urban nature.

Looking strictly at the positioning the female graves as compared with their counterparts at Kaupang gives us no basis for gender based social differentiation. They are found in the same cemeteries, in the same kind of positions, with similar wealth, sometimes in the same grave, and very often next to each other. Oseberg presents a picture such as many other contemporary monumental burials give, positioned on a plain, a free standing, lonely monument which draws attention to itself, due to its size and its unique position. Had we not had such heavy reliance on our preconceived ideas of Late Iron Age gender structuring in Norway, would we, from this evidence, have drawn the conclusions that we tend to do, or would we instead have concluded that we were looking at a cultural tradition of more gender fluidity than what is often afforded the popular image of the Viking Age?

Some of the female gendered graves at Kaupang do indeed stand out from their male counterparts, in terms of outer shape as remarked in Chapter 5. These are the long mounds, which are particularly well documented at Nordre Kaupang (Blindheim 1981f:93). As mentioned in chapter five, there are women buried in all the different types of burial manifested at Kaupang. Thus, the long barrows cannot be said to be a definite female marker, in that we know women could be buried with other types of outer markings, and indeed without any outer markings. The long barrows at Nordre Kaupang are found intermingled with male burials, and their location does not appear to stand out in any way. If we assume that gender can be coded in the landscape (Kearney 2008:25), the question of why this different outer shape was chosen, and who merited it becomes interesting. I suggest that the different outer shape may mean they were meant to be seen, and that this was on account of the social significance or specific role of the individuals buried in them. At this stage, it is difficult to state anything of use in terms of what this role was, but it is tempting to speculate in the fact that there are two of these graves found with remains of iron staffs (see Appendix for details). Other than this though, the material does not give any indication of a ritual role, and I will be content at this stage with raising questions which can be further explored. The excavated long mounds at Nordre Kaupang which yielded finds that allowed gendering were all female (Blindheim 1981d:93). These mounds all gave relatively rich finds. The outer shape also means they were distinctive to the passer by. The question then becomes: were they gender coded? Were they meant to show the presence of a certain type of person? And if so, was this class of person always female?

At this point, it seems prudent to look to the sources that testify that men and women filled different social functions, and that there were known punishments for crossing over these (Lia 2002:305). It was a humiliating and shameful act for a man to act like a woman, known as ergi (Lia 2002:305; Solli 1999:396), but for a woman to act like a man was often a positive: a woman who displayed masculine traits was often accorded honour (Solli 1999:396). It is interesting to observe these conventions, which hint towards greater leniency being afforded women than men in terms of their social roles. By accounts given in written sources, male and female roles were segregated, but the leader of the gods, Odin, was known to indulge in 'female' activities, seen for example in his knowledge and practice of seið (Solli 1999:423). Other gods such as the male Loke displays complex, even confusing, gender fluidity, in his shape shifting and by even giving birth (Solli 1999:420). Can we perhaps read from this a more fluid gender ideology than what has previously been suggested?

Moreover, we cannot be sure how much we can trust the written sources available, and as archaeologists, I believe we must allow archaeological evidence to take precedence if there have doubts. Looking at material evidence in the form of grave goods, we find some interesting occurrences of apparent gender fluidity, as mentioned in Chapter 1. Artefacts connected with textile production (such as weaving swords or spindle whorls) are traditionally thought of as female accoutrements, but are not unheard of in male graves. At Kaupang, there are male graves with textile tools, and even one with a trefoil brooch, which are normally associated with female assemblages (see Appendix for further detail). There have also been male burials noted containing oval brooches (Rygh 1999 [1985]:33).

In the same way there have been finds made of female graves with weapons, equestrian equipment and other 'male' markers such as weights (Blindheim and Heyerdahl-Larsen 1995c:128; Lia 2001:83; Pedersen 2000:16). One of the most concrete examples of cross-over graves in terms of gendered artefacts is a female grave found at Nordre Kjølen by Flisa in Hedmark, which was discovered with a full set of weapons, that is sword, axe, shield boss, arrow heads, a spearhead, a hone and other items (Lia 2002:308-309). Full sets of weapons like the one found at Nordre Kjølen are often seen as unequivocally male. In the case of this burial however, the skeletal remains showed this to be a woman. Speculations on the social role of this woman will not be included here, but it remains an interesting example of gender fluidity in terms of artefact categories.

Another such interesting find is the female burial at Gausel, near Stavanger in Rogaland county. A rich grave gendered as female, this contained the customary female artefacts: oval brooches and other jewellery, bronze vessels and beads, but also a large array of more traditional male artefacts, such as a substantial amount of equestrian equipment, and a shield boss (Børseng 1997:3). There was also a 'roasting spit', or possible volve staff found in this burial (ibid), which provides a possible ritual link. The burial is dated to around 850 A.D, which sets it close to Oseberg in terms of chronology, although geographically, these two burials are quite far apart.

In the Oseberg burial there is also some evidence of gender fluidity, in the saddle which is found as part of the grave goods. Equestrian equipment is as mentioned above often seen as male, yet here it is found in a double female burial, yet another pointer to that we must expect variations in gender patterns.

Both of the two above mentioned burials might provide interesting comparisons to the Oseberg burial. This does not come under the scope of this study however, and so will not be pursued further here. One reason for this is that the study aims to stay focused on a small area in terms of geography. It is also felt that it is important to keep the focus here on landscape and strategic positioning, and so we will not go further down this route of grave goods at the moment.

It seems the arguments are becoming more and more persuasive for us to open up discussion on gender roles in the Viking Age once more, and perhaps move away from our earlier, narrow interpretations. I wish to suggest that we may need to assess the possibility that the strict gender roles which we are accustomed to ascribing to the Late Iron Age may be more an ideal representation in textual sources than a true reflection of reality, and that reality was made up by a more complex gender pattern than the idealised public male and private female.

6.6 Conclusion

This chapter has aimed to show how we can widen our lines of enquiry, and subsequently potentially our understanding of gender constructions in the Viking

Chapter 6: Discussion

Age through the careful study of mortuary remains, both in terms of positioning in the landscape and through the actual material remains we are faced with. These two sides of the evidence are inextricably linked, and should be interpreted as a whole.

I conclude that we have compelling evidence for further study, in order to establish whether a stronger social position for women than what has often been suggested in academic interpretations needs to be established. A cultic role need not mean complete removal from the political sphere. Similarly, a role in the household need not mean segregation from public administration.

Chapter 7. Conclusion

This chapter will serve as a conclusion to the foregoing discussions and arguments and will thus present the final notes to be made on the subject discussed in the previous chapters.

After conducting the research for this study, it is my belief that the careful study of the topographical positioning of graves can further expand our understanding of social order in the Viking Age. As I hope has been made apparent in the foregoing chapters, there is persuasive evidence that the graves of the Viking Age show no gender based differentiation in terms of positioning, at least not in the evidence which has been examined here. Drawing on the arguments outlined throughout this study, and allowing that place and position was a consideration for people of the Viking Age when they chose where to deposit their dead, I believe this lack of gender differentiation is significant.

Accepting that the people of the Viking Age saw men and women as different categories, need not mean they were socially differentiated to a degree which was detrimental to one sex as a general rule, as I believe has been shown by the relative positioning of graves in the landscape. Ruling the home need not equate to a hidden and passive role merely because that is the common value coding of such a role in recent western society (Arwill-Nordblad 1998:47). It could mean a platform for power and influence on a different, but equivalent level available to men (Hoftun 1995:110). What can be seen in the reflection of mortuary tradition on the landscape appears to reaffirm the fact that women and men shared the social arena. I do not believe we can continue to argue for women on the margins when faced with clear evidence in the form of manifestations in the landscape of women buried alongside men, in the same types of locations, and with the same types of material remains as well as remains of the same types of rituals. This recalls the argument that a symbol gains its meaning by common association, and thus identical monuments are likely to carry the same meaning. Repetition is partly what makes a ritual potent, and it appears logical to apply the same rules of interpretation to burials of a similar nature.

The higher number of male gendered graves compared to female graves may indicate that the roles which entitled individuals to a highly visible burial may have been more easily available to men. But there are alternative explanations which could be considered: as was discussed in the introduction to this study, the archaeological gendering of graves carries some inherent dangers in terms of potentially disregarding gender-ambiguous graves. The potential for misidentification of gender or sex on the basis of personal adornment or costume (Arnold 2002:241) cannot be ignored, and we must always be aware of this when dealing with empirical evidence which has, in the main, been gendered on archaeological grounds. Of course, the sheer lack of skeletal remains from the Late Iron Age in Norway presents a problem in terms of sex and gender determination in alternative ways, but this means we must be cautious in throwing about numbers and statistics when the evidence is not of a definite nature. Further, I would draw attention to the arguments presented in Chapter 6, on the subject of lack of 'female' markers in graves, and how this may be attributable to other causes than a lack of socially active women. Excavation methods must be examined, along with archaeological methods for gendering graves. The lack of differentiation in the landscape lends strength to this argument.

These arguments should not be confused with imposing a model of complete gender equality, or of searching for matriarchy in the past. It is not my aim to glorify Viking Age women and make assertions about their ultimate gender equality. Indeed, as has been argued by others before me, it ought to be possible to acknowledge that women in the past may have had access to power without immediately jumping to suggestions of matriarchy (Fuglestvedt 2006:54; Jesch 1994:25). I merely wish to point to the very clear similarities of women and men's positions in the mortuary landscape, and pose the question of whether we ought to allow for more social fluidity and room for individual agency in our interpretations of the past, rather than turn to sweeping generalisations of past social structure and gender roles which leave little room for ideological and geographical variation. It may be that we need to modify our ideas of fierce warrior men, and authoritarian, but sidelined, women. This model is unfair both to men and to women, and disregards individual personalities and ambitions for both genders. It also forgets the complex power play which is to be expected from any culture and society. It ought to be allowed that in a society where women were known to have strong influence, if not direct authority (Dommasnes 1998:342), they would not in all circumstances have been bound by the same strict rules of domesticity which we have become accustomed to throughout our own recent history (Arwill-Nordbladh 1998:39). It remains a distinct possibility that the 'influence' often afforded to women of the Late Iron Age was of a more public and overt nature than what we would now assign to the role of an influential housewife. The 'private' sphere of the house and farm might not have been considered in the same light in the Viking Age, and might have been more in the public arena than in the private (Gräslund 2001:83).

I believe the landscape can be used to broaden our understanding of past social constructs, and it may be appropriate to accept a higher degree of social fluidity in the Viking Age. The next natural step would be to extend the study of topographical positioning of graves to inland areas and different types of communities. Unfortunately, there has not been room in this study to

Chapter 7: Conclusion

take this further, but it presents an interesting prospect for further study. I believe this may hold potential for giving a more balanced view of who was afforded what type of social visibility in death, and by continuing this line of enquiry, there is potential for increasing our understanding of past gender roles.

The Gendered Landscape

Cat. No	Museum No	Name	Location	External shape	Grave type	Body treatment	Gender	Artefacts	Date	Reference
Ka.1	C4198 – 4203	Nicolaysen's barrow 47	N. Kaupang	Barrow	Boat grave?	Cremation	Male	Double-edged sword, spearhead, axe soapstone vessel, copper alloy ring-pin, hone, textiles, stone, 20 rivets	900 - 950	Stylegar 2007:104; Lia 2001: appendix 5; Hofseth 1999
Ka. 2	C4204 – 4204	Nicolaysen's barrow 109	N. Kaupang	Barrow		Cremation	Male	Sword, sword?, axe	850 – 950	Stylegar 2007:104; Lia 2001: appendix 5
Ka. 3	C4206 – 4215	Nicolaysen's barrow 113	N. Kaupang	Barrow (Long barrow)		Cremation	Female	2 oval brooches, 2 beads (1 cornelian?), iron saucepan, iron frying pan, iron spit?, spindle-whorl, looped hone, 2 sickles, axe, horse bit, rivet, iron rod, iron cauldron?, iron rattle	900 – 950	Stylegar 2007:104; Lia 2001: appendix 5; Hofseth 1999
Ka. 4	C4216 – 4224	Nicolaysen's barrow 112	N. Kaupang	Barrow	Boat grave?	Cremation	Male	Double-edged sword, double-edged sword, spearhead, axe, boss, sickle, weight (spherical), weight (cubo-octaedric), copper alloy key, soapstone vessel, 2 hones, egg-shaped stone, 4 flints, c. 20 rivets	900 – 950	Stylegar 2007:104; Lia 2001:appendix 5
Ka. 5	C4225	Nicolaysen's barrow 10	N. Kaupang	Barrow		Cremation		Pottery (Slavonic), 1 bolt, 6 rivets	800 – 900?	Stylegar 2007:104; Lia 2001:appendix 5
Ka. 6	C4226 - 4234	Nicolaysen's barrow 90	N. Kaupang	Barrow		Cremation	Male	Double-edged sword, iron rattle, spearhead, axe, 3 bosses, copper alloy scales, weight (cubooctaedric), sickle, at least 2 soapstone	900 – 950	Stylegar 2007:104; Lia 2001:appendix 5

Table

								vessels, several hones, flints, scissors, horse bit, 2 rivets, axe, iron handle attachment, knife?, iron mount, iron plate (from cauldron?), pieces of iron		
Ka. 7	C4235 – 4236	Nicolaysen's barrow 92	N. Kaupang	Barrow		Cremation	Male	Boss, horse bit, cruciform mount of iron, iron fragments, soapstone vessel, double-edged sword?, arrowhead?, sickle?	900 – 950	Stylegar 2007:104; Lia 2001:appendix 5
Ka. 8	C4237 – 4243	Nicolaysen's barrow 91	N. Kaupang	Barrow		Cremation	Male	Sword, spearhead, axe, boss, arrowhead, copper alloy scales, 3 weights (spherical), weight (unknown type), copper alloy ring-pin, copper alloy bell, soapstone vessel, several hones, flints, iron handle, horse bit, knife?, sickle?	900 – 950?	Stylegar 2007:104; Lia 2001:appendix 5
Ka. 9	C4244	Nicolaysen's barrow 84	N. Kaupang	Barrow		Cremation		Pieces of iron frying pan or cauldron, rivet, horse bit, egg-shaped stone, iron socket, pieces of iron		Stylegar 2007:104; Lia 2001:appendix 5
Ka. 10	C4245 – 4251	Nicolaysen's barrow 85	N. Kaupang	Barrow (long barrow)		Cremation	Female	2 oval brooches, 2 beads (glass), spindle-whorl of soapstone, axe, sickle, soapstone vessel, iron sword beater, horse bit, iron hook, casket handle, iron rod, rectangular iron mount, hone, 2 - 3 rivets	900 - 1000	Stylegar 2007:104; Lia 2001:appendix 5 ; Hofseth 1999

The Gendered Landscape

Ka. 11	C4252 - 4253	Nicolaysen's barrow 18	N. Kaupang	Barrow		Cremation		Axe, 2 soapstone vessels, fragmentary iron cauldron, rivets, sickle, scissors	900 – 950	Stylegar 2007:104; Lia 2001:appendix 5
Ka. 12	C4254	Nicolaysen's barrow 19	N. Kaupang	Barrow	Boat Grave ?	Cremation		4 rivets		Stylegar 2007:104; Lia 2001:appendix 5
Ka. 13	C4255	Nicolaysen's barrow 26	N. Kaupang	Barrow		Cremation	Male	Sickle, Iron rod, 11 rivets, iron rod (tang for arrowhead?), fragmentary iron cauldron, spearhead		Stylegar 2007:104, Lia 2001:appendix 5
Ka. 14	C4256 - 4259	Nicolaysen's barrow 94	N. Kaupang	Barrow (long barrow)		Cremation	Female	Iron sword-beater, iron handle, sherds of pottery (tatinger ware), rivets, horse bit, sickle	800 - 900?	Stylegar 2007:104; Lia 2001:appendix 5
Ka. 15	C4260	Nicolaysen's barrow 100	N. Kaupang	Barrow		Cremation		Hone, iron rivet		Stylegar 2007:104; Lia 2001:appendix 5
Ka. 16	C4261 – 4265	Nicolaysen's barrow 77	N. Kaupang	Barrow (long barrow)		Cremation	Female	2 oval brooches, textiles, iron sword-beater, scissors, spindle-whorl of burnt clay, axe, sickle, horse bit, (harness) mount	900 – 950	Stylegar 2007:106; Lia 2001:appendix 5; Hofseth 1999
Ka. 17	C4266	Nicolaysen's barrow 11	N. Kaupang	Barrow		Cremation	Male	Fragment of natural stone		Stylegar 2007:106; Lia 2001:appendix 5
Ka. 18	C4267	Nicolaysen's barrow 57	N. Kaupang	Barrow		Cremation		Rivet, pieces of iron		Stylegar 2007:106; Lia 2001:appendix 5
Ka. 19	C4268	Nicolaysen's barrow 35	N. Kaupang	Barrow		Cremation		Spearhead, iron fragment	900 – 1000	Stylegar 2007:106; Lia 2001:appendix 5
Ka.	C4269	Nicolaysen's	N. Kaupang	Barrow		Cremation		Adze, 2 rivets		Stylegar

Table

20		barrow 70								2007:106; Lia 2001:appendix 5
Ka. 21	C4270	Nicolaysen's barrow 69	N. Kaupang	Barrow	Boat Grave ?	Cremation		Fragmentary iron cauldron, arrowhead, 1 or 2 iron socket, iron ring, iron file?, fragmentary iron mount, hone, several rivets		Stylegar 2007:106; Lia 2001:appendix 5
Ka. 22	C4271 - 4275	Nicolaysen's barrow 60	N. Kaupang	Barrow (Long barrow)		Cremation	Female	Bead (glass), iron sword-beater, soapstone vessel, sickle, horse bit, iron escutcheon, rim mount for iron cauldron?, rivet or bolt, iron fragment, iron brace, spearhead?, spherical stone	900 - 1000?	Stylegar 2007:106; Lia 2001:appendix 5
Ka. 23		Nicolaysen's barrow 16	N. Kaupang	Barrow		Cremation		Soapstone vessel	900 – 1000?	Stylegar 2007:106
Ka. 24		Nicolaysen's barrow 28	N. Kaupang	Barrow		Cremation		Rivets		Stylegar 2007:106
Ka. 25		Nicolaysen's barrow 32	N. Kaupang	Barrow		Cremation		Rivet		Stylegar 2007:106
Ka. 26		Nicolaysen's barrow 33	N. Kaupang	Barrow		Cremation		2 rivets		Stylegar 2007:106
Ka. 27		Nicolaysen's barrow 36	N. Kaupang	Barrow		Cremation		Sword		Stylegar 2007:106
Ka. 28		Nicolaysen's barrow 41	N. Kaupang	Barrow		Cremation		Iron fragments		Stylegar 2007:106
Ka. 29		Nicolaysen's barrow 45	N. Kaupang	Barrow		Cremation		Pottery		Stylegar 2007:106
Ka. 30		Nicolaysen's barrow 48	N. Kaupang	Barrow		Cremation		Rivets		Stylegar 2007:106
Ka. 31		Nicolaysen's barrow 52	N. Kaupang	Barrow		Cremation		Rivets		Stylegar 2007:106
Ka. 32		Nicolaysen's barrow 59	N. Kaupang	Barrow		Cremation		Rivets, iron fragments		Stylegar 2007:106
Ka. 33		Nicolaysen's barrow 64	N. Kaupang	Barrow		Cremation		Rivets		Stylegar 2007:106

The Gendered Landscape

Ka. 34		Nicolaysen's barrow 83	N. Kaupang	Barrow		Cremation		Soapstone vessel		Stylegar 2007:106
Ka. 35		Nicolaysen's barrow 86	N. Kaupang	Barrow		Cremation		Rivets		Stylegar 2007:106
Ka. 36		Nicolaysen's barrow 114	N. Kaupang	Barrow	Boat Grave	Cremation		c. 50 rivets		Stylegar 2007:106
Ka. 37	K/XXIII, K/XXI Vd		N. Kaupang	Barrow?	Boat grave	Cremation	Male	Double-edged sword, adze, iron cauldron, boss, at least 6 arrowheads, 2 sickles, 2-3 iron keys, 2 iron hooks, pottery (Tating ware), pottery (Badorf ware) mosaic tesserae, 4 beads, hone, iron slag, pieces of iron, rivets, nails, axe	850 - 900	Stylegar 2001:106; Lia 2001:appendix 5
Ka. 38		Nicolaysen's barrow 25	N. Kaupang	Barrow				Empty barrow		Stylegar 2007:106
Ka. 39		Nicolaysen's barrow 37	N. Kaupang	Barrow				Empty barrow		Stylegar 2007:106
Ka. 40		Nicolaysen's barrow 43	N. Kaupang	Barrow				Empty barrow		Stylegar 2007:108
Ka. 41		Nicolaysen's barrow 51	N. Kaupang	Barrow				Empty barrow		Stylegar 2007:108
Ka. 42		Nicolaysen's barrow 54	N. Kaupang	Barrow				Empty barrow		Stylegar 2007:108
Ka. 43		Nicolaysen's barrow 66	N. Kaupang	Barrow				Empty barrow		Stylegar 2007:108
Ka. 44		Nicolaysen's barrow 99	N. Kaupang	Barrow				Empty barrow		Stylegar 2007:108
Ka. 45		Nicolaysen's barrow 110	N. Kaupang	Barrow?				Empty barrow		Stylegar 2007:108
Ka. 46		Nicolaysen's barrow 5	N. Kaupang	Barrow				Layers or patches of charcoal		Stylegar 2007:108
Ka. 47		Nicolaysen's barrow 9	N. Kaupang	Barrow				Layers or patches of charcoal		Stylegar 2007:108
Ka. 48		Nicolaysen's barrow 12	N. Kaupang	Barrow				Layers or patches of charcoal		Stylegar 2007:108

Table

Ka. 49		Nicolaysen's barrow 13	N. Kaupang	Barrow				Layers or patches of charcoal		Stylegar 2007:108
Ka. 50		Nicolaysen's barrow 14	N. Kaupang	Barrow				Layers or patches of charcoal		Stylegar 2007:108
Ka. 51		Nicolaysen's barrow 15	N. Kaupang	Barrow				Layers or patches of charcoal		Stylegar 2007:108
Ka. 52		Nicolaysen's barrow 17	N. Kaupang	Barrow				Layers or patches of charcoal		Stylegar 2007:108
Ka. 53		Nicolaysen's barrow 27	N. Kaupang	Barrow				Layers or patches of charcoal		Stylegar 2007:108
Ka. 54		Nicolaysen's barrow 30	N. Kaupang	Barrow				Layers or patches of charcoal		Stylegar 2007:108
Ka. 55		Nicolaysen's barrow 34	N. Kaupang	Barrow				Layers or patches of charcoal		Stylegar 2007:108
Ka. 56		Nicolaysen's barrow 38	N. Kaupang	Barrow				Layers or patches of charcoal		Stylegar 2007:108
Ka. 57		Nicolaysen's barrow 40	N. Kaupang	Barrow				Layers or patches of charcoal		Stylegar 2007:108
Ka. 58		Nicolaysen's barrow 49	N. Kaupang	Barrow				Layers or patches of charcoal		Stylegar 2007:108
Ka. 59		Nicolaysen's barrow 50	N. Kaupang	Barrow				Layers or patches of charcoal		Stylegar 2007:108
Ka. 60		Nicolaysen's barrow 53	N. Kaupang	Barrow				Layers or patches of charcoal		Stylegar 2007:108
Ka. 61		Nicolaysen's barrow 55	N. Kaupang	Barrow				Layers or patches of charcoal		Stylegar 2007:108
Ka. 62		Nicolaysen's barrow 56	N. Kaupang	Barrow				Layers or patches of charcoal		Stylegar 2007:108
Ka. 63		Nicolaysen's barrow 58	N. Kaupang	Barrow				Layers or patches of charcoal		Stylegar 2007:108
Ka. 64		Nicolaysen's barrow 65	N. Kaupang	Barrow				Layers or patches of charcoal		Stylegar 2007:108
Ka. 65		Nicolaysen's barrow 72	N. Kaupang	Barrow				Layers or patches of charcoal		Stylegar 2007:108
Ka. 66		Nicolaysen's barrow 73	N. Kaupang	Barrow				Layers or patches of charcoal		Stylegar 2007:108
Ka. 67		Nicolaysen's barrow 74	N. Kaupang	Barrow				Layers or patches of charcoal		Stylegar 2007:110
Ka.		Nicolaysen's	N. Kaupang	Barrow				Layers or		Stylegar

68		barrow 75						patches of charcoal		2007:110
Ka. 69		Nicolaysen's barrow 76	N. Kaupang	Barrow				Layers or patches of charcoal		Stylegar 2007:110
Ka. 70		Nicolaysen's barrow 93	N. Kaupang	Barrow				Layers or patches of charcoal		Stylegar 2007:110
Ka. 71		Nicolaysen's barrow 105	N. Kaupang	Barrow				Layers or patches of charcoal		Stylegar 2007:110
Ka. 72		Nicolaysen's barrow 106	N. Kaupang	Barrow				Layers or patches of charcoal		Stylegar 2007:110
Ka. 73		Nicolaysen's barrow 115	N. Kaupang	Barrow				Layers or patches of charcoal		Stylegar 2007:110
Ka. 125	C4317		Hagejordet	Barrow		Inhumation		Glass pseudo-cameo inlay, axe	800 - 900	Stylegar 2007:110; Lia 2001:appendix 5
Ka. 126	K/XXX V	Nicolaysen's barrow 1?	Hagejordet	Barrow (round)	Boat grave	Cremation	Female	Equal armed silver brooch (unica?), c. 20 beads, copper alloy tweezers, weight (spherical), sheet copper alloy, 3 - 4 bone combs, iron hinge, rivets, slag	900 - 1000	Stylegar 2007:110; Lia 2001:appendix 5
Ka. 127	K/XXX VI	Nicolaysen's barrow 2?	Hagejordet	Barrow	Boat grave	Cremation		Bead (glass), spherical lead object, knife, iron point, rectangular iron mount, iron fragments, iron strike-a-light?, rivets, nails, slag, cremated animal bone		Stylegar 2007:110; Lia 2001:appendix 5
ka. 128	K/XXI Va		Hagejordet	Casual find				Copper alloy thistle brooch		Stylegar 2007:110
Ka. 129	K/XXI Vb		Hagejordet	Casual find				Copper alloy arm ring, textiles (wool)	800 - 850	Stylegar 2007:110
Ka. 130	K/XXII		Hagejordet	Flat grave?	Boat grave	Cremation		2 horse bits, sickle, 2 - 3 beads (glass), rivets, nails		Stylegar 2007:110; Lia 2001:appendix 5
Ka. 131	C22309 a		Hagejordet	Casual find				Axe		Stylegar 2007:110; Lia 2001:appendix 5
Ka. 132	C22309 b		Hagejordet	Casual find				Copper alloy bracelet		Stylegar 2007:110
Ka. 133	Lost find		Hagejordet	Casual find				Rivets		Stylegar 2007:110
Ka. 134	C54272		Hagejordet	Casual find				Iron ring		Stylegar 2007:110
Ka. 150	C2270 - 2280 I		S. Kaupang	Barrow		Cremation		Single-edged sword, axe, boss, spearhead	800 - 850	Stylegar 2007:110

Table

Ka. 151	C2270 - 2280II		S. Kaupang	Barrow		Cremation		Sword, copper alloy thistle brooches - symmetric animal style, 2 soapstone vessels, (weapon knife?, bead (glass), scythe, adze, hone, rivets, nails, iron file?, piece of iron - these objects derive from either of the two graves in this barrow)	900 - 950	Stylegar 2007:110
Ka. 152		Nicolaysen's barrow 1	S. Kaupang	Barrow		Cremation		Rivets		Stylegar 2007:110
Ka. 153	C4286	Nicolaysen's barrow 2	S. Kaupang	Barrow		Cremation		Spearhead, arrowhead, 3 - 4 rivets	900 - 950	Stylegar 2007:110
ka. 154	C4287 - 4288	Nicolaysen's barrow 4	S. Kaupang	Barrow		Cremation		Bead (glass), spindle whorl of stone, rivet		Stylegar 2007:110
ka. 155	C4289 - 4290	Nicolaysen's barrow 5	S. Kaupang	Barrow		Cremation		Copper alloy key, sherds of pottery (Rinish)		Stylegar 2007:110
Ka. 156	C4291 - 4292	Nicolaysen's barrow 7	S. Kaupang	Barrow		Cremation		Iron forging hammer, hone, rivets, sword?		Stylegar 2007:112
Ka. 157	C4293 - 4315	Nicolaysen's barrow 6	S. Kaupang	Barrow	Boat grave?	Cremation		Double-edged sword, spearhead, axe, boss, 2 arrowheads, iron rattle, 2 stirrups, copper alloy horse bit, copper alloy swivel (from a dog lead?), copper alloy bell, copper alloy button from a horse harness?, copper alloy animal's head from a horse harness?, sickle, 2 knives, iron rasp, iron spoon auger, iron tool, 2 iron hasps for a chest (iceberg type), 2 pieces of sheet iron, iron lock spring iron rod, iron key?, iron mount, iron hinge, iron clamp, fragmentary	800 - 850	Stylegar 2007:112

								iron cauldron, at least 12 rivets, object of whalebone, hone, ornate iron mount (from a sword?), 4 curved iron pieces, iron ring with clamp, scythe, 2 fishing hooks, spearhead, fragmentary shield grip?, iron handle, iron rod, several iron pieces		
Ka. 158		Nicolaysen's barrow 8	S. Kaupang	Barrow		Cremation		Rivets		Stylegar 2007:112
Ka. 159		Nicolaysen's barrow 9	S. Kaupang	Barrow		Cremation		Rivets		Stylegar 2007:112
Ka. 160	C15214 - 15218		S. Kaupang	Barrow	Boat grave	Cremation		Double-edged sword, knife, strike-a-light with copper alloy mount (symmetric animal style), sickle, hasp, key, fragmentary iron cauldron, lock mount, mount for chest (type Oseberg), handle for iron cauldron, scutcheon, key?, hook-shaped iron object, iron bolt, rivets	850 - 900	Stylegar 2007:112
Ka. 161	C15219		S. Kaupang	Barrow				Fragments of 1 or 2 oval brooches	800 - 850	Stylegar 2007:112; Hofseth 1999
ka. 162			S. Kaupang	Barrow				Empty barrow		Stylegar 2007:112
Ka. 163			S. Kaupang	Barrow				Indeterminable iron objects, rivets		Stylegar 2007:112
Ka. 164			S. Kaupang	Barrow				Indeterminable iron objects, rivets		Stylegar 2007:112
Ka. 165	C33255		S. Kaupang	Barrow (the object may or not derive from Ka. 163 or Ka 164)				Axe	900 - 950	Stylegar 2007:112
Ka. 166	Lost find		S. Kaupang	Flat grave?		Cremation		Scissors		Stylegar 2007:112

Table

Ka. 167	Lost find	Kristensen's A390	S. Kaupang	Barrow				Iron fragments, soapstone fragments, hone		Stylegar 2007:112
Ka. 200	C5508 - 5509		Lamøya	Flat grave?				Soapstone vessel, spearhead?, flint?	900 - 1000	Stylegar 2007:112
Ka. 201	C15010 - 15011		Lamøya	Flat grave		Cremation		Double-edged sword, soapstone vessel	900 - 1000	Stylegar 2007:112
Ka. 202	C17719 - 17722		Lamøya	Flat grave		Cremation		Spearhead, axe, axe, soapstone vessel, rivet	900 - 950	Stylegar 2007:112
Ka. 203	C21843, 21960	Gustafson's barrow 1	Lamøya	Barrow	Boat grave	Inhumation	Female	2 oval brooches, textiles, equal-armed silver brooch, strike-a-light, Thor's hammer?, strap buckle, escutcheon, knife, rivets, nails, fishing hook, 8 beads (7 glass, 1 cornelian)	800 - 900	Stylegar 2007:112; Hofseth 1999; Lia 2001:appendix 5
Ka. 204	C21960 I		Lamøya		Boat grave with cremated bones	Cremation	Male	Spearhead, 2 arrowheads, knife, iron spoon auger, sickle, scissors, file, iron fragment, arrowhead?, handle attachment for wooden bucket, iron hook, arrowhead?, sherds of pottery, 4 beads (glass), stave from wooden bucket, fragmentary oak keel-plank from a boat, c. 240 rivets, 2 oval hammer-stones, flint nodule, iron fragments	800 - 900	Stylegar 2007:112
Ka. 205	C21960 II	Gustafson's barrow 2	Lamøya	Barrow		Cremation		Piece of iron, horse bit, rivets, glass stave, 5 beads		Stylegar 2007:112
Ka. 206	C27148		Lamøya	Flat grave?		Inhumation		Soapstone vessel, 3 beads (glass), iron cauldron		Stylegar 2007:112
Ka. 207			Lamøya	Flat grave				Lost find: sword, 2 axes, several brooches, 3 hones		Stylegar 2007:112

Ka. 208	C27220 (Grave 1)		Lamøya	Flat grave		Inhumation		Sword, axe, axe, boss, copper alloy penanular brooch, 2 hones		Stylegar 2007:112
Ka. 209	C27220 (graveII)		Lamøya	Flat grave			Male	Axe	850 - 950	Stylegar 2007:112
Ka. 210	C27220 (grave III)		Lamøya	Flat grave		Inhumation	Female	2 oval brooches, textiles, horse-shaped copper alloy brooch, copper alloy needle case	800 - 850	Stylegar 2007:112; Hofseth 1999; Lia 2001:appendix 5
Ka. 211	C31482		Lamøya	Casual find				Axe, textiles	950 - 1000	Stylegar 2007:112
Ka. 212			Lamøya	Casual find				Soapstone vessel	900 - 1000	Stylegar 2007:114
Ka. 213			Lamøya	Casual find				Spearhead		Stylegar 2007:114
Ka. 214			Lamøya	Casual find				Sword, spearhead, 2 axes, soapstone vessel	900 - 1000	Stylegar 2007:114
Ka. 215			Lamøya	Casual find				Soapstone vessel, rivets	900 - 1000	Stylegar 2007:114
Ka. 216	K/XXVII		Lamøya	Casual find				Sword	800 - 950	Stylegar 2007:114
Ka. 217	K/XXXIX	Gurihaugen	Lamøya	Barrow				Empty barrow		Stylegar 2007:114; Lia 2001:appendix 5
Ka. 218	K/X	Dortehaugen	Lamøya	Barrow		Inhumation	Female	Jet ring, bead (glass), bone gaming piece, spindle-whorl, iron needle, sickle-shaped cutting tool, tongue shaped strike-a-light, 2 iron rings, rivet, clamp, hook, wooden remains of floorboard, dog rib, c. 180 rivets	850 - 900	Stylegar 2007:114
Ka. 219	K/XXVII		Lamøya	Flat grave		Inhumation	Female	2 oval brooches, cruciform insular copper alloy mount, 8 beads (glass), soapstone vessel, iron frying pan, iron key, sickle, small iron ball, one or more knives, rivet, undeterminable iron fragments, iron slag,	850 - 950	Stylegar 2007:114; Hofseth 1999; Lia 2001:appendix 5

Table

								wooden cask, textiles		
Ka. 220	Lost find		Lamøya	Casual find				Sword		Stylegar 2007:114
Ka. 221	C54296/1		Lamøya	Casual find				Insular mount		Stylegar 2007:114
Ka. 222	C54290/1		Lamøya	Casual find				Silver dirham		Stylegar 2007:114
Ka. 223	Lost find		Lamøya	Casual find				Soapstone vessel		Stylegar 2007:114
Ka. 224	Lost find		Lamøya	Casual find				Sword		Stylegar 2007:114
Ka. 225	C54290/2		Lamøya	Casual find				Sword		Stylegar 2007:114
Ka. 226	C54290/3		Lamøya	Casual find				Sword		Stylegar 2007:114
Ka. 227			Lamøya	Casual find				3 beads (glass)		Stylegar 2007:114
Ka. 228	C54292/1		Lamøya	Casual find				Sword		Stylegar 2007:114
Ka. 229			Lamøya	Lost find from barrow				Rivets etc		Stylegar 2007:116
Ka. 230		Gustafson's barrow 3	Lamøya	Barrow				Rivets etc		Stylegar 2007:116
Ka. 250	C27740 A, K/XXI VG?		Bikjholberget	Flat grave	Boat grave, double grave	Inhumation	Female	2 oval brooches, textiles, equal-armed brooch, insular strap buckle with copper alloy mount, double-edged sword, spearhead, scythe, spindle-whorl of soapstone, horseshoe, c. 160 rivets, scissors, knife, iron key, animal bone, (copper alloy key), (horse), (copper alloy trefoil brooch)	800 - 900	Stylegar 2007:116; Hofseth 1999; Lia 2001:appendix 5
Ka. 251	C27740 B		Bikjholberget	Flat grave	Boat grave			Oval brooch	800 - 900	Stylegar 2007:116; Lia 2001:appendix 5; Hofseth 1999
Ka. 252	C27997 grave A		Bikjholberget	Flat grave	Boat grave	Inhumation	Male	Double-edged sword, sword?, spearhead, axe, boss, 8 arrowheads, knife, knife?, strike-a-light, scissors, knife, knife, lock, 2	900 - 950	Stylegar 2007:116; Lia 2001:appendix 5

								knives?, fishing hook, pieces of iron, soapstone sinker, 5 beads (4 glass, 1 amber), 7 flints, c. 135 nails and rivets, animal teeth, soapstone vessel		
Ka. 253	C27997 grave B		Bikjholberget	Flat grave	Boat grave	Inhumation	Female	3 oval brooches, textiles, iron sword-beater, soapstone vessel, boss, arrowhead, soapstone vessel, hone, rivets (insular mount of gilt copper alloy?)	800 - 900	Stylegar 2007:116; Lia 2001:appendix 5; Hofseth 1999
Ka. 254	C27997 grave C		Bikjholberget	Flat grave	Boat grave	Inhumation	Female	2 oval brooches, copper alloy equal-armed brooch, copper alloy rectangular brooch, 4 copper alloy arm rings, copper alloy chain from necklace, copper alloy spiral from necklace copper alloy cord, textiles, copper alloy ring, 18 beads (13 glass, 4 amber, 1 silver), sickle, arrowhead?, knife	800 - 850	Stylegar 2007:116; Lia 2001:appendix 5; Hofseth 1999
Ka. 255	K/1950 grave 1		Bikjholberget	Flat grave	Boat grave, possibly in same boat as Ka. 254	Inhumation	Male	Double-edged sword, spearhead, iron sword-beater, boss, iron handle, boss?	800 - 85-	Stylegar 2007:116; Lia 2001:appendix 5
Ka. 256	k/1950 grave II		Bikjholberget	Flat grave	Boat grave?	Inhumation	Male	Double-edged sword, spearhead, kesselgabel, boss, boss?, crampon, hone	900 - 950	Stylegar 2007:116; Lia 2001:appendix 5
Ka. 257	K/1950 grave III		Bikjholberget	Flat grave	Boat grave	Inhumation	Male	Double-edged sword, spearhead, boss, knife/arrowhead, 2 scissors, lock with scutcheon, iron hinge, looped needle case,	900 - 950	Stylegar 2007:116; Lia 2001:appendix 5

Table

								tweezers, strike-a-light, needle hone, sword?, spearhead?, scythe		
Ka. 258	K/1950 Grave IV		Bikjholberget	Flat grave	Boat grave, in same as Ka. 257	Inhumation	Male	Sword, spearhead	900 - 1000	Stylegar 2007:116; Lia 2001:appendix 5
Ka. 259	K/1950 Grave V		Bikjholberget	Flat grave	Boat grave, probably in same boat as Ka. 257-58	Inhumation	Female	Copper alloy coin brooch, copper alloy fragments (oval brooch?), knife, needle hone, iron cauldron? Bowl, soapstone vessel, sickle, textiles	900 - 1000	Stylegar 2007:116; Lia 2001:appendix 5; Hofseth 1999
Ka. 260	K/1950 grave VI		Bikjholberget	Flat grave	?	Inhumation		Sword, (knife?), (fishing hook?)	900 - 1000	Stylegar 2007:116; Lia 2001:appendix 5
Ka. 261	K/1950 grave VII		Bikjholberget	Flat grave	?	Inhumation		Axe, boss, tang, cork, iron fragments	850 - 950	Stylegar 2007:116; Lia 2001:appendix 5
Ka. 262	K/1952 grave1		Bikjholberget	Flat grave	Boat grave, double grave (infant)	Inhumation	Male	Double-edged sword, axe, knife, boss, leather purse?, rivets, weight?	900 - 95-	Stylegar 2007:116; Lia 2001:appendix 5
Ka. 263	K/1952 grave II		Bikjholberget	Flat grave	Boat grave		Male	Sword, spearhead?, (axe?), (2 beads?)	900 - 950	Stylegar 2007:118; Lia 2001:appendix 5
ka. 264	K/1954 grave IV		Bikjholberget	Flat grave	Boat grave, possibly in same boat as Ka. 263			Sword, spearhead, adze, knife, sickle, mount for casket?, strike-a-light, copper alloy ring-pin, 2 small insular copper alloy objects, copper alloy button, ornament of copper alloy or silver, 3 pieces of silver, 2 tongue-shaped mounts of sheet copper alloy (strap ends?), 2 soapstone vessels, (axe?) (forging hammer?), (needle hone?)	800 - 900	Stylegar 2007:118; Lia 2001:appendix 5

The Gendered Landscape

Ka. 265	K/1953 grave I		Bikjholberget	Flat grave	Boat grave	Inhumation	Female	2 oval brooches, 2 beads (rock crystal), spindle-whorl, knife, slag?, iron fragment?, textile	800 - 850	Stylegar 2007:118; Lia 2001:appendix 5; Hofseth 1999
Ka. 266	K/1953 grave VIII		Bikjholberget	Flat grave	Boat grave, possibly in same boat as Ka. 265	Inhumation	Male	Sword	800 - 950	Stylegar 2007:118; Lia 2001:appendix 5
ka. 267	K/1953 grave II		Bikjholberget	Flat grave	Boat grave, seated burial?	Inhumation	Female	2 oval brooches, feathers/down, equal armed brooch, 10 beads, 37 rivets, textiles	800 - 850	Stylegar 2007:118; Lia 2001:appendix 5; Hofseth 1999
Ka. 268	K/1953 grave III		Bikjholberget	Flat grave	Boat grave	Inhumation	Female	2 oval brooches, copper alloy rectangular strap buckle, rectangular insular book mount of copper alloy, copper alloy needle, 19 beads (glass), spindle whorl, 2 knives, 14 rivets, textiles	800 - 850	Stylegar 2007:118; Lia 2001:appendix 5; Hofseth 1999
Ka. 269	K/1953 grave IV		Bikjholberget	Flat grave	Log coffin	Inhumation	Female	Axe, knife, pottery, 4 nails	800 - 850	Stylegar 2007:118; Lia 2001:appendix 5
ka. 270	K/1953 grave V		Bikjholberget	Flat grave	Chamber with coffin	Inhumation	Male	Sword, adze, sickle/scythe, hone, brooch, 4 beads, spearhead, hone, bolt, lock mount, knife, hand-made pottery (North sea type), rivets, smoothing stone?, textiles (gold thread), animal teeth, trefoil brooch	900 - 950	Stylegar 2007:118; Lia 2001:appendix 5
Ka. 271	K1953 grave V		Bikjholberget	Flat grave	Wooden coffin	Inhumation		axe, knife, knife, animal teeth	900 - 950	Stylegar 2007:118; Lia 2001:appendix 5
ka. 272	K1953 grave VI		Bikjholberget	Flat grave	Boat grave	Inhumation	Male	Axe, knife, oval brooch?, fragment of pottery, needle hone, bead (glass), penannular copper alloy brooch, tongue-shaped strike-a-light with	850 - 900	Stylegar 2007:118; Lia 2001:appendix 5; Hofseth 1999

Table

								copper alloy mount			
ka. 273	K/ 1953 grave VII		Bikjholberget	Flat grave	Boat grave?	Inhumation	Male	Sword	800 - 950	Stylegar 2007:118; Lia 2001:appendix 5	
Ka. 274			Bikjholberget	Flat grave	Grave without coffin	Inhumation		Skeleton		Stylegar 2007:118; Lia 2001:appendix 5	
Ka. 275			Bikjholberget	Flat grave	Grave without coffin	Inhumation		Skeleton		Stylegar 2007:118; Lia 2001:appendix 5	
Ka. 276			Bikjholberget	Flat grave	Grave without coffin	Inhumation		Skeleton		Stylegar 2007:118; Lia 2001:appendix 5	
Ka. 277	K/1954 grave I	Felt Veien Albertina	Bikjholberget	Flat grave	Boat grave	Inhumation	Male	Sword, spearhead, boss, knife, spearhead, sickle, penannular iron brooch, clamp, rivets, soapstone vessel, glass sherd (from beaker?), rivets and nails	950 - 1000	Stylegar 2007:118; Lia 2001:appendix 5	
Ka. 278	K/1954 grave II	Felt Veien	Bikjholberget	Flat grave	Log coffin	Inhumation	Male	Sword, spearhead, adze, knife, penannular copper alloy brooch, hone	850 - 950	Stylegar 2007:118; Lia 2001:appendix 5	
Ka. 279	K/1954 grave III	Felt fjellet	Bikjholberget	Flat grave	Boat grave	Inhumation	Male	Sword, spearhead, boss, knife, copper alloy bucket-tongue, hone, flint, 2 long nails, rivets, bead (glass), indeterminable iron pieces	900 - 950	Stylegar 2007:120; Lia 2001:appendix 5	
Ka. 280	K/1954 grave V	Felt Veien	Bikjholberget	Flat grave	Chamber grave?	Inhumation	Male	Cruciform silver pendant, 7 beads (5 glass, 2 amber), knife, arrowhead, iron object, silver coin	900 - 1000	Stylegar 2007:120; Lia 2001:appendix 5	
Ka. 281	K/1954 grave VI	Felt Veien	Bikjholberget	Flat grave	Chamber grave? Ka. 280 and Ka. 282 may or may not constitute one grave	Inhumation	Female	Axe, scythe, knife, handle, flint, 2 beads (1 glass), needle hone, soapstone vessel, mount for a casket, hone, rivets and nails	900 - 1000?	Stylegar 2007:120; Lia 2001:appendix 5	

ka. 282	K/1954 grave VII	Felt Veien	Bikjholberget	Flat grave	Boat grave	Inhumation	Female	Spearhead, axe, knife, crampon, 2 mounts shaped like miniature adzes, hook, flint, hook and mount for casket, spindle-whorl, burnt wood, 2 beads, 2 weight (spherical), rivets (knife?), (bone spindle-whorl?) (Soapstone spindle-whorl?)	900 - 1000	Stylegar 2007:120; Lia 2001:appendix 5
Ka. 283	K/1954 VIII	Felt fjellet	Bikjholberget	Flat grave	Boat grave	Inhumation	Female	3 oval brooches, copper alloy drinking horn mount, soapstone vessel, loom weight, textiles	850 - 950	Stylegar 2007:120; Hofseth 1999; Lia 2001:appendix 5
ka. 284	K/1954 IX	Felt Fjellet	Bikjholberget	Flat grave	Boat grave, seated burial?	Inhumation	Female	2 oval brooches, axe, axe, knife, spindle-whorl, 3 beads (1 glass, 2 amber), spindle-whorl, fragmentary glass beaker, textiles, animal teeth	900 - 950	Stylegar 2007:120; Lia 2001:appendix 5; Hofseth 1999
Ka. 285	K/1954 grave X	Felt fjellet	Bikjholberget	Flat grave	Boat grave	Inhumation	Female	2 oval brooches, axe, iron cauldron, soapstone vessel, key, small ring, mount from casket, knife, scissors, needle hone, soapstone vessel, knife, knife, handle, knife, indeterminable piece of iron, 2 beads (glass), spindle-whorl of amber, mount, heckle?, textiles	900 - 950	Stylegar 2007:120; Lia 2001:appendix 5; Hofseth 1999
ka. 286	K/1954 Grave XI	Felt fjellet	Bikjholberget	Flat grave	Boat grave (same as Ka. 284)	Inhumation	Female	2 oval brooches, trefoil brooch, trefoil brooch, 2 beads (1	850 - 900	Stylegar 2007:120; Lia 2001:appendix 5;

Table

								amber, 1 cornelian), belt buckle, belt buckle, 2 hones, 3 soapstone fragments, rivets, textiles		Hofseth 1999
Ka. 287	K/1954 Grave XII	Felt fjellet	Bikjholberget	Flat grave	Boat grave (same as Ka. 284)	Inhumation	Male	Spearhead, adze, 2 iron gaffs, knife, knife, lead sinker, hone, bead, soapstone vessel	800 - 850	Stylegar 2007:120; Lia 2001:appendix 5
Ka. 288	K/1954 grave XIII	Felt Veien	Bikjholberget	Flat grave	?	Inhumation		Rivets		Stylegar 2007:120; Lia 2001:appendix 5
Ka. 289			Bikjholberget	Flat grave	Boat grave, heavily disturbed	Inhumation		Skeleton		Stylegar 2007:120; Lia 2001:appendix 5
ka. 290	K/1	Maihaugen	Bikjholberget	Flat grave	Stone cist	Inhumation	Male	Hand-made pottery (North-sea type), arrowhead, iron tool, socket for arrowhead / javelin, rivet, nails, 2 iron rods, piece of amber, flint	800 - 900?	Stylegar 2007:120; Lia 2001:appendix 5
Ka. 291	K/II	Kosmos	Bikjholberget	Flat grave	Boat grave	Inhumation	Female	Oval brooch, textiles, trefoil brooch, sickle, knife, 2 keys, iron mount, 2 animal teeth, c. 240 rivets and nails	c. 900?	Stylegar 2007:120; Lia 2001:appendix 5; Hofseth 1999
Ka. 292	K/III grave I	Ormen Lange	Bikjholberget	Flat grave	Boat grave	Inhumation	Male	2 spearheads, axe, boss, sickle, knife, plane tool, 2 iron awls?, scraper tool of iron, iron shaft, iron handle for wooden bucket soapstone vessel, iron fragments, 2 hones, bead (glass), piece of clay, flint, pottery sherds	900 - 950	Stylegar 2007:120; Lia 2001:appendix 5
Ka. 293	K/III grave II	Ormen Lange	Bikjholberget	Flat grave	Boat grave	Inhumation	Male	Spearhead, 4 arrowheads, knife, lead capsule (reliquary), copper alloy belt buckle, c. 500 rivets and nails, 3 iron brackets, horse	c. 800?	Stylegar 2007:120; Lia 2001:appendix 5

								skeleton		
Ka. 294	K/IV grave I	Forargelsens Hus	Bikjholberget	Flat grave, four sided stone setting	Boat grave, double grave	Inhumation	Female	2 gilded oval brooches, textiles, trefoil brooch, silver ring, 29 beads (glass), silver bracelet, iron handle, 2 iron rods, iron sword-beater, key, knife, ring (horse bit?), animal teeth	900 - 950	Stylegar 2007:122; Lia 2001:appendix 5; Hofseth 1999
Ka. 295	K/IV grave II	Forargelsens Hus	Bikjholberget	Flat grave, four sided stone setting	Boat grave	Inhumation	Male	Sword, axe, adze, javelin / arrowhead, at least 4 arrowheads, boss, scythe, iron frying pan / saucepan, soapstone vessel, arrowhead, hone, iron object (horse-?dog collar?) 2 spindle-whorls, pottery, 3 beads (glass), 2 knives, 2 nails, rivet, horse skeleton, strap end, strap plate, plate with pin through, 32 small copper alloy coated iron rivets, horse bit	900 - 10000	Stylegar 2007:122; Lia 2001:appendix 5
Ka. 296	K/IV grave III	Forargelsens Hus	Bikjholberget	Flat grave, four sided stone setting	Boat grave, seated burial?	Inhumation	Female	2 oval brooches, copper alloy basin with runic inscription, copper alloy ring with clamp, tweezer shaped copper alloy object with one arm, gilt copper alloy rod, iron sword-beater, iron staff, axe, horse bit, iron rod, 5 beads (glass), egg-shaped stone, hone, hand-made pottery, boss, sheet iron,	850 - 950	Stylegar 2007:122; Lia 2001:appendix 5; Hofseth 1999

Table

								fragments of wood and bark, 2 iron brackets, dog skeleton		
Ka. 297	K/IV grave IV	Forargelsens Hus	Bikjholberget	Flat grave	Below the boat	Inhumation	Male	Spearheads, penannular brooch of lead / iron / tin, strike-a-light, 2 flints, iron objects (tool?), 2 knives, egg-shaped stone, sherds of soapstone vessel, hone	800 - 850	Stylegar 2007:122; Lia 2001:appendix 5
Ka. 298	K/V grave I	Forargelsens Hus II	Bikjholberget	Flat grave	Boat grave, double burial	Inhumation	Male	Sword, forging hammer, forging tong, sickle, spearhead, adze, boss, knife, 2 copper alloy ring-pins, round insular mount of gilt copper alloy with spiral ornaments, insular mount of gilt copper alloy, 4 beads (2 glass, 2 amber), soapstone vessel, iron gaff, looped hone, flint, knife, textiles	900 - 1000	Stylegar 2007:122; Lia 2001:appendix 5
Ka. 299	K/V grave II	Forargelsens Hus II	Bikjholberget	Flat grave	Boat grave	Inhumation	Female	Equal-armed brooch of copper alloy, copper alloy arm ring, copper alloy ring from necklace, 22 beads (18 glass, 1 rick crystal, 1 cornelian, 2 amber), miniature spearhead, axe, key, 2 knives, spindle-whorl, iron fragments	800 - 850	Stylegar 2007:122; Lia 2001:appendix 5
Ka. 300	K/V grave III	Forargelsens Hus II	Bikjholberget	Flat grave	Boat grave	Inhumation	Male	Single-edged sword, axe, insular mount of gilt copper alloy, knife, 2 rivets, nails, knife?, hone, strike-a-light, indeterminable iron fragments, c. 850 rivets and nails	850 - 950	Stylegar 2007:122; Lia 2001:appendix 5

Ka. 301	K/VI grave II	Najaden	Bikjholberget	Flat grave	Boat grave	Inhumation	Male	Double-edged sword, spearhead, knife, weight (spherical), ring-pin of copper alloy, 3 beads (2 amber, 1 jet), spindle-whorl, handmade pottery, glass sherd	860 - 900	Stylegar 2007:122; Lia 2001:appendix 5
Ka. 302	K/VI grave II	Najaden	Bikjholberget	Flat grave	Boat grave	Inhumation	Male	Spearhead, axe, sickle, scissors, 3? Knives, casket? Mount, iron object (sword beater?), looped hone, crampon, indeterminable iron fragments, c. 240 rivets and nails, one piece of cremated bone	900	Stylegar 2007:122; Lia 2001:appendix 5
Ka. 303	K/VII Grave I	Rosshavet	Bikjholberget	Flat grave	Boat grave	Inhumation	Female	Oval brooch, equal armed brooch, axe, sickle, 7 - 8 beads (4 glass, 1 amber), sickle, 5 knives, lead sinker, arrowhead, hone, spindle-whorl, iron fragments (2 knives)	875 - 900	Stylegar 2007:122; Lia 2001:appendix 5; Hofseth 1999
Ka. 304	K/VII Grave II	Rosshavet	Bikjholberget	Flat grave	Boat grave	Inhumation	Female	2 oval brooches, insular mount of gilt copper alloy, 3 beads (glass), 2 copper alloy fragments, 5 sherds of glass, handmade pottery, knife, flint nodule with bent nail, flint nodule with iron ring, egg-shaped stone, textiles. The following objects could derive from any of the graves in Rosshavet: Iron fragments, 2 egg-shaped stones, 2 slag,	800 - 850	Stylegar 2007:122; Lia 2001:appendix 5; Hofseth 1999

Table

								flint, c. 500 rivets and nails. The following objects found under Ka/ 301 may or may not derive from Rosshavet: weight, jet bead, pottery, glass sherd		
Ka. 305	K/VIII	Skibladner	Bikjholberget	Flat grave	Boat grave	Inhumation	Male	Double-edged sword, spearhead, axe, boss, arrowheads, 7 beads (6 glass, 1 stone), sickle, knife, handmade pottery, 3 glass sherds, rivets, nails, 2 flints, silver coin?, pumice, animal skeleton, animal horn and bone, animal teeth, c. 450 rivets and nails.	c/ 900	Stylegar 2007:124; Lia 2001:appendix 5
Ka. 306		Martine	Bikjholberget	Flat grave	Boat grave		Male	Pottery, round insular copper alloy mount, silver ring, fragments of amber (bead?), spindle-whorl	800 - 900	Stylegar 2007:124; Lia 2001:appendix 5
Ka. 307	K/IX	Sistemann	Bikjholberget	Flat grave	Boat grave with chamber	Inhumation	Male	Sword, copper alloy belt buckle, bead (cornelian), strap buckle of iron, mount piece of iron (for belt / sword?), indeterminable iron fragments, knife, looped hone, smoothing stone, c. 250 rivets	850 - 950	Stylegar 2007:124; Lia 2001:appendix 5
Ka. 308	K/XI	Thorshøvdi	Bikjholberget	Flat grave	Boat grave	Inhumation	Male	Spearhead, boss, copper alloy needle, 7 beads (glass), sickle, file?, knife, iron cauldron, hone, knife?, silver coin?, indeterminable iron fragments, c 250 rivets and	900 - 950	Stylegar 2007:124; Lia 2001:appendix 5

								nails, button, textiles		
Ka. 309	K/XVII grave II	Smertensbarnet	Bikjholberget	Flat grave	Boat grave	Inhumation	Male	Double-edged sword, spearhead, spearhead, axe, bronze ring-pin, forging tong, hammer, 3 knives, soapstone vessel, handle, strap buckle of iron for horse harness, bead (glass), horse bit, arrowheads, 2 bolts c. 200 rivets and nails, c. 40 g of cremated human and animal bones, weapon knife, boss, pieces of wood from the boat, textiles	900-95-	Stylegar 2007:124; Lia 2001:appendix 5
Ka. 310	K/XIII grave II	Britannia	Bikjholberget	Flat grave	Boat grave	Inhumation	Female	2 oval brooches, horse shaped copper alloy brooch, 57 beads (56 glass, 1 amber), rectangular mount, iron rod, pottery (bar lip pottery), spindle-whorl, fragmentary sickle, escutcheon, wooden bucket	800-900	Stylegar 2007:124; Lia 2001:appendix 5; Hofseth 1999
Ka. 311	K/XIII grave II	Britannia	Bikjholberget	Flat grave	Boat grave	Inhumation	Male	9? Arrowheads, knife, iron chain, bark, burnt stone, c. 130 rivets and nails, double-edged sword, knife, axe, copper alloy ring-pin, wooden cup	800-900	Stylegar 2007:124; Lia 2001:appendix 5
Ka. 312	K/XXV		Bikjholberget	Flat grave	Boat grave	Inhumation	Male	Double-edged sword, round brooch of gilt copper alloy, rivet, indeterminable iron fragments, bead (glass)	900-950	Stylegar 2007:124; Lia 2001:appendix 5
Ka. 313	K/XVI	Astrids kiste	Bikjholberget	Flat grave	Toboggan/trough	Inhumation		Sickle, knife, key, 23 nails		Stylegar 2007:124;

Table

					sled			and rivets		Lia 2001:appendix 5
ka. 314	K/XVIII		Bikjholberget	Flat grave	Toboggan/trough sled	Inhumation		Knife, 9 rivets		Stylegar 2007:124; Lia 2001:appendix 5
ka. 315	K/XIV	Ringen	Bikjholberget	Flat grave	Wooden coffin	Inhumation	Male	Spearhead, 2 beads (amber), soapstone vessel, glass stave, soapstone sinker, c. 50 nails and rivets, mount piece of iron / scuthceon, copper alloy needle, textiles	800 - 900	Stylegar 2007:124; Lia 2001:appendix 5
Ka. 316	K/XV	Pulterkammeret	Bikjholberget	Flat grave	Chest (type Oseberg) double grave (child	Inhumation	Male	Spearhead, 2 bosses, iron cauldron, scutcheon, hinges from casket, file?, knife, 12 rivets and nails, hone. Objects found in secondary position, trefoil brooch, sickle, iron hook, fishing hook, knife, indeterminable iron fragments, 2 hinges?, bead (glass), a piece of cremated bone	850 - 900	Stylegar 2007:124; Lia 2001:appendix 5
Ka. 317	K/XXI	Pulterkammeret	Bikjholberget	Flat grave		Horse grave		The horse grave Ka 317 probably belongs to Ka. 316: carved horse skeleton, horse bit, 1 iron nail with gilt copper alloy coated head, 5 iron nails, cruciform iron mount, adze, flint, arrowhead, 2 rectangular iron plates	850 - 900	Stylegar 2007:124; Lia 2001:appendix 5
Ka. 318	K/XVII	Charlottes kiste	Bikjholberget	Flat grave	Wooden coffin			Bead (glass), iron nails, flint		Stylegar 2007:124; Lia 2001:appendix 5
Ka. 319	K/XXXVII	Wenckes kiste	Bikjholberget	Flat grave	Wooden coffin			2 nails		Stylegar 2007:124; Lia 2001:appendix 5

ka. 320	K/XXXVIII	Randis kiste	Bikjholberget	Flat grave	Wooden coffin			Wooden cup, 2 nails		Stylegar 2007:124; Lia 2001:appendix 5
Ka. 321	K/XIX		Bikjholberget	Flat grave		Inhumation	Male	Spearhead, axe, 2 beads (1 amber, 1 stone), knife, indeterminable iron fragments	900 - 950	Stylegar 2007:126; Lia 2001:appendix 5
Ka. 322	K/XX		Bikjholberget	Flat grave	Wooden coffin	Inhumation	Male	Double-edged sword, knife, c. 10 nails	800 - 850	Stylegar 2007:126; Lia 2001:appendix 5
Ka. 323	K/XXVII		Bikjholberget	Flat grave	?	Inhumation		Rivets, flint, animal teeth, cremated bone		Stylegar 2007:126; Lia 2001:appendix 5
Ka. 400	C2317 I		N. Kaupang	Barrow		Cremation		Oval brooch	800 - 850	Stylegar 2007:126; Lia 2001:appendix 5; Hofseth 1999
Ka. 401	C2317 II		N. Kaupang	Barrow		Inhumation		Two oval brooches	850 - 950	Stylegar 2007:126; Hofseth 1999
Ka. 402	C2317 III		N. Kaupang	Barrow		Inhumation		Axe		Stylegar 2007:126
Ka. 403	C4070		N. Kaupang	Flat grave		Inhumation		Single-edged sword	830/840 - 900	Stylegar 2007:126; Lia 2001:appendix 5
Ka. 404	C4316		N. Kaupang	Casual find				Stone sinker		
Ka. 405	C14678		N. Kaupang	Barrow				Spearhead		Stylegar 2007:126
Ka. 406	C30264		Kaupang	Flat grave?		Cremation		2 oval brooches, trefoil copper alloy brooch, conical copper alloy button, 12 beads (11 glass, 1 cornelian), spindle-whorl, soapstone vessel	850 - 950	Stylegar 2007:126; Hofseth 1999
Ka. 407	C30265		Kaupang	Barrow		Inhumation		axe, sword pommel	850 - 950	Stylegar 2007:126
	1950		Bikjholberget	Collection of casual finds				2 beads (glass), round stone, spindle-whorl of soapstone, spindle-whorl of stone, 2 spindle whorls of fired clay, ring, triangular clamp, needle case of iron,		Stylegar 2007:126

							copper alloy ring, hinge?, rod		
	1951		Bikjholberget	Collection of casual finds				Fragments of soapstone, hone, spindle-whorl? bead of jet, spindle-whorl / bead of amber, loom weight of fired clay, flint, horse bit, c 60 rivets and nails, piece of bone		Stylegar 2007:126
	1952		Bikjholberget	Collection of casual finds				Thorn from insular ring-pin, 6 beads (3 glass, 2 amber, 1 rock crystal), flywheel of soapstone, knife, arrowhead, slag, flint, loom weight? of fired clay		Stylegar 2007:126
	1953		Bikjholberget	Collection of casual finds				Axe, knife, sickle, bundle of sowing needles, iron fragment, round copper alloy pendant, knife, slag, knife/sickle, bead (glass), scissors, knife? 2 ring-pins		Stylegar 2007:126
	1954		Bikjholberget	Collection of casual finds				Sword, sword, axe, sickle, spearhead, iron object, oval brooch, spindle-whorl of fired clay, spindle whorl of stone, hone, 2 soapstone vessels		Stylegar 2007:126

Bibliography

Arnold, Bettina, and Nancy L. Wicker 2001 Introduction. In *Gender and the Archaeology of Death* edited by Bettina Arnold and Nancy L. Wicker, pp. Vii – xxi. Altamira Press, Walnut Creek.

Arnold, Bettina 2002 Sein und Werden: Gender as Process in Mortuary Ritual. In *In Pursuit of Gender* edited by Nelson, Sarah Milledge, and Myriam Rosen-Ayalon, pp. 239–256. Altamira Press, Oxford.

Arwill–Nordbladh, Elisabeth 1998 *Genuskonstruksjoner i Nordisk Vikingatid: Förr och nu.* Gotarc Gothenburgh Archaeological Press, Göthenburg.

Ashmore, Wendy 2007 Social archaeologies of Landscape. In *A Companion to Social Archaeology*, edited by Meskell, Lynne, and Robert W. Preucel, pp. 259–271. Blackwell, Malden.

Bakken, Asbjørn 1959 *Kongshaugen på Gokstad.* Sandefjord Sjøfartsmuseum, Sandefjord.

Bertelsen, Reidar, Grete Lillehammer, and Jenny-Rita Næss (eds.) 1987 *Were They All Men? An Examination of Sex Roles in Prehistoric Society.* AmS – Varia Vol. 17, Stavanger Museum of Archaeology, Stavanger.

Birkeli, Emil 1943 *Fedrekult: Fra Norsk folkeliv i hedensk og kristen tid.* Dreyer Forlag, Oslo.

Blake, Emma 2007 Space, Spatiality and Archaeology. In *A Companion to Social Archaeology*, edited by Meskell, Lynne, and Robert W. Preucel, pp. 230–254. Blackwell, Malden.

Blindheim, Charlotte 1981a Gravskikk. Gruppe 1b. Nicolaysens material. In *Kaupang-funnene. Bind 1* by Blindheim, Charlotte, Birgitte Heyerdahl-Larsen, and Roar L. Tollnes, pp.73– 83. Universitetets Oldsaksamling, Oslo.

Blindheim, Charlotte 1981b Gravskikk, gruppe 1a Løsfunn og tilfeldige gravninger. In *Kaupang-funnene. Bind 1* by Blindheim, Charlotte, Birgitte Heyerdahl-Larsen, and Roar L. Tollnes, pp. 85– 89. Universitetets Oldsaksamling, Oslo.

Blindheim, Charlotte 1981c Gravskikk. Sammenfatning. In *Kaupang-funnene. Bind 1* by Blindheim, Charlotte, Birgitte Heyerdahl-Larsen, and Roar L. Tollnes, pp. 91–92. Universitetets Oldsaksamling, Oslo.

Blindheim, Charlotte 1981d Gravenes Innhold: generelle Betraktninger. In *Kaupang-funnene. Bind 1* by Blindheim, Charlotte, Birgitte Heyerdahl-Larsen, and Roar L. Tollnes, pp. 93–107. Universitetets Oldsaksamling, Oslo.

Blindheim, Charlotte 1981e Båtgravskikken. In *Kaupang-funnene. Bind 1* by Blindheim, Charlotte, Birgitte Heyerdahl-Larsen, and Roar L. Tollnes, pp. 109–114. Universitetets Oldsaksamling, Oslo.

Blindheim, Charlotte 1981f Gravenes Innhold: sammmenfatning. In *Kaupang-funnene. Bind 1* by Blindheim, Charlotte, Birgitte Heyerdahl-Larsen, and Roar L. Tollnes, pp. 115–125. Universitetets Oldsaksamling, Oslo.

Blindheim, Charlotte et al. 1981 Katalog med plansjer. In *Kaupang-funnene. Bind 1* by Blindheim, Charlotte, Birgitte Heyerdahl-Larsen, and Roar L. Tollnes, pp. 199–223. Universitetets Oldsaksamling, Oslo.

Blindheim, Charlotte 1995a Innledning. In *Kaupangfunnene, Bind II. Gravplassene Bikjholberget / Lamøya. Undersøkelsene 1950 – 57* by Blindheim, Charlotte and Birgit Heyerdahl-Larsen, pp. 9– 14. Universitetets Oldsaksamling, Oslo.

Blindheim, Charlotte 1995b Gjennomgang av N. Bikjholberget. In *Kaupangfunnene, Bind II. Gravplassene Bikjholberget / Lamøya. Undersøkelsene 1950 – 57* by Blindheim, Charlotte and Birgit Heyerdahl-Larsen, pp. 55–87. Universitetets Oldsaksamling, Oslo.

Blindheim, Charlotte and Birgit Heyerdahl-Larsen 1995a Gravskikk, sammenfatning av kapitlene 3 og 4. In *Kaupangfunnene, Bind II. Gravplassene Bikjholberget / Lamøya. Undersøkelsene 1950 – 57* by Blindheim, Charlotte and Birgit Heyerdahl-Larsen, pp. 113–114. Universitetets Oldsaksamling, Oslo.

Blindheim, Charlotte. And Birgit Heyerdahl-Larsen 1995b De døde. In *Kaupangfunnene, Bind II. Gravplassene Bikjholberget / Lamøya. Undersøkelsene 1950 – 57* by Blindheim, Charlotte and Birgit Heyerdahl-Larsen, pp. 115–126. Universitetets Oldsaksamling, Oslo.

Blindheim, Charlotte and Birgit Heyerdahl-Larsen 1995c Rituelle trek, magi – spor av Kristen innflytelse. In *Kaupangfunnene, Bind II. Gravplassene Bikjholberget / Lamøya. Undersøkelsene 1950 – 57* by Blindheim, Charlotte and Birgit Heyerdahl-Larsen, pp. 127–184. Universitetets Oldsaksamling, Oslo.

Bourdieu, Pierre 1996 *Symbolsk Makt.* Pax Forlag, Oslo.

Brink, Stefan 2007 How Uniform was the Old Norse religion? In *Learning and Understanding in the Old Norse World*, edited by Quinn, Judy, Kate Heslop, and Tarrin Wills, pp. 105–136. Brepols, Turnhout.

Brink, Stefan 2008 Landskap och plats som mentala konstruksjoner. In *Facets of Archaeology; Essays in honour of Lotte Hedeager on her 60th birthday* edited by Childis, Konstantinos, Julie Lund, and Christopher Prescott, pp. 109–120. Oslo Arkeologiske Serie, Vol. 10, Unipub, Oslo.

Brøgger, Anton Wilhelm 1916 *Borrefundet og Vestfoldkongernes Graver.* A. W. Brøggers Boktrykkeri: Kristiania.

Brøgger, Anton Wilhelm 1921 *The Oseberg Ship.* Universitetets Oldsaksamling, Oslo.

Brøgger, Anton Wilhelm, HJ. Falk, and Haakon Shetelig (eds.) 1917 *Osebergfundet. Bind I.*

Bibliography

Published by the Norwegian Government, Universitetets Oldsaksamling, Kristiania.

Børseng, Ragnar L. 1997 Nye undersøkelser av Gauseldronningens grav. In *Frá haug ok heiðni* 4. Pp. 3 – 10.

Casey, Edward S. 2008 Place in Landscape Archaeology: A Western Philosophical Prelude. In *Handbook of Landscape Archaeology* edited by David, Bruno, and Julian Thomas, pp. 44–51. Left Coast Press, Walnut Creek.

Christensen, Arne Emil 1987 *Husfruen på Oseberg*. Vestfold Historielag, Vestfold.

Christensen, Arne Emil, Anne Stine Ingstad, and Bjørn Myhre 1993 Introduksjon. In *Osebergdronningensgrav. Vår arkeologiske nasjonalskatt i nytt lys,* by Christensen, Arne Emil, Anne Stine Ingstad, and Bjørn Myhre, pp. 7–9. Schibsted, Oslo.

Christensen, Arne Emil 1993a Aldri har noen arkeolog fått en slik femtiårsgave. In *Osebergdronningensgrav. Vår arkeologiske nasjonalskatt i nytt lys,* by Christensen, Arne Emil, Anne Stine Ingstad, and Bjørn Myhre, pp. 51–66. Schibsted, Oslo.

Christensen, Arne Emil 1993b Gravleggingen. In *Osebergdronningensgrav. Vår arkeologiske nasjonalskatt i nytt lys,* by Christensen, Arne Emil, Anne Stine Ingstad, and Bjørn Myhre, pp. 80–84. Schibsted, Oslo.

Christensen, Arne Emil 1993c Kongsgårdens håndverkere. In *Osebergdronningensgrav. Vår arkeologiske nasjonalskatt i nytt lys,* by Christensen, Arne Emil, Anne Stine Ingstad, and Bjørn Myhre, pp. 85–137. Schibsted, Oslo.

Christensen, Arne Emil 1993d Skipet. In *Osebergdronningensgrav. Vår arkeologiske nasjonalskatt i nytt lys,* by Christensen, Arne Emil, Anne Stine Ingstad, and Bjørn Myhre, pp. 138–153. Schibsted, Oslo.

Conkey, Margaret W, and Janet D. Spector 1998 Archaeology and the Study of Gender. In *Reader in Gender Archaeology,* edited by Hays–Gilpin, Kelley, and David S.Whitley, pp. 11–45. Routledge, London.

Darvill, Timothy 2008 Pathways to a Panoramic Past: A Brief History of Landscape Archaeology in Europe. In *Handbook of Landscape Archaeology* edited by David, Bruno, and Julian Thomas, pp. 60–77. Left Coast Press, Walnut Creek.

David, Bruno and Julian Thomas 2008 Landscape Archaeology: Introduction. In *Handbook of Landscape Archaeology* edited by David, Bruno, and Julian Thomas, pp. 27–44. Left Coast Press, Walnut Creek.

Dommasnes, Liv Helga 1994 Tradisjon og endring belyst gjennom forhistorisk materiell kultur – en skisse. In *Myte og Ritual i det Førkristne Norden: et symposium,* edited by Schjødt, Jens Peter, pp. 25–40. Odense Universitets Forlag, Odense.

Dommasnes, Liv Helga 1998 Women, Kinship, and the Basis of Power in the Norwegian Viking Age. In *Reader in Gender Archaeology,* edited by Hays–Gilpin, Kelley, and David S.Whitley, pp. 337–345. Routledge, London.

Dommasnes, Liv Helga, Else Johansen Kleppe, Gro Mandt and Jenny-Rita Næss 1998 Women Archaeologists in retrospect: The Norwegian case. In *Excavating Women: A History of Women in European Archaeology* edited by Díaz-Andreu, Margarita, and Marie Louise Stig Sørensen, pp. 105–125. Routledge, London.

Doucette, Dianna L. 2001 Decoding the Gender Bias: Inferences of Atlatls in Female Mortuary Contexts. In *Gender and the Archaeology of Death* edited by Bettina Arnold, and Nancy L. Wicker, pp. 159 – 177. Altamira Press, Walnut Creek.

Engesveen, Anne 2005 *På Vei Mellom Levende og Døde*. Unpublished Masters dissertation. Universitetet i Oslo, Oslo.

Fahlander, Fredrik 2006 Kön och gender som seriekollektiv: Sosiala aspekter på korporealitet och handling. In *Det Arkeologiske Kjønn* edited by Skogstrand, Lisbeth, and Ingrid Fuglestvedt, pp. 27–42. Oslo Arkeologiske Serie Vol. 7, Unipub, Oslo.

Forseth, Lars 1993 *Vikingtid i Østfold og Vestfold: En kildekritisk gransking av regionale forskjeller i gravfunnene.* Unpublished Masters dissertation. Universitetet i Oslo, Oslo.

Fowler, Chris 2008 Landscape and Personhood. In *Handbook of Landscape Archaeology* edited by David, Bruno, and Julian Thomas, pp. 291–299. Left Coast Press, Walnut Creek.

Fuglestvedt, Ingrid 1997 Mellom hedendom og kristendom – mellom ættesamfunn og kongerike: Bruken av monumentale anlegg i en brytningstid. In *Konflikt i Forhistorien* edited by Fuglestvedt, Ingrid, and Bjørn Myhre, pp. 41–57. AmS-Varia Vol. 30, Stavanger Museum of Archaeology, Stavanger.

Fuglestvedt, Ingrid 2006 Matriarkatet – mellom det mulige ureele og det mulige: Noen tanker omkring forholdet mellom kvinnedyrkelse, feminisme og kjønnsarkeologi. In *Det Arkeologiske Kjønn* edited by Skogstrand, Lisbeth, and Ingrid Fuglestvedt, pp. 43–62. Oslo Arkeologiske Serie Vol. 7, Unipub, Oslo.

Gansum, Terje 1995 *Jernaldergravskikk i Slagendalen. Oseberghaugen og Storhaugene i Vestfold. Lokale eller regionale symboler: En landskapsarkeologisk undersøkelse.* Unpublished dissertation for magister degree. Universitetet i Oslo, Oslo.

Gansum, Terje 1996 Borrehaugene på ny i støpeskjeen – tanker omkring storhaugene i Vestfold. In *Borreminne. Lokalhistorie fra Borre og*

Horten 12, pp. 9–20. Borre Historielag, Horten.

Gansum, Terje 1997 Jernaldermonumenter og maktstrukturer: Vestfold som konfiktarena. In *Konflikt i Forhistorien* edited by Fuglestvedt, Ingrid, and Bjørn Myhre, pp. 27–40. AmS-Varia Vol. 30, Stavanger Museum of Archaeology, Stavanger.

Gansum, Terje 1999 Mythos, Logos, Ritus – Symbolisme og gravskikk i lys av gudediktene i den elder Edda. In *Et hus med mange rom: Vennebok til Bjørn Myhre på 60 års dagen. Bind B*, edited by Fuglestvedt, Ingrid, Terje Gansum, and Arnfrid Opedal, pp. 441–504. AmS rapport Vol. 11, Stavanger Museum of Archaeology, Stavanger.

Gansum, Terje 2004 *Hauger som Konstruksjoner – arkeologiske forventninger gjennom 200 år.* GOTARC Series B, Vol. 33, Gothenburg archaeological theses, Gothenburg University, Department of Archaeology, Gothenburgh.

Gansum, Terje and Bjørn Myhre 2003 *Borrefunnet 1852 – 2002*. Midgard historiske senter Midgard forlag, Horten.

Gansum, Terje, Per Holck, and Vivian Wangen 2008 *Ny Viten om Gokstad-høvdingen.* Sandar Historielag, Sandefjord.

Gilchrist, Roberta 1999 *Gender and Archaeology: Contesting the Past.* Routledge, London

Gilchrist, Roberta 2007 Archaeology and the Life Course: A Time and Age for Gender. In *A Companion to Social Archaeology*, edited by Meskell, Lynne, and Robert W. Preucel, pp. 142–160. Blackwell, Malden.

Grieg, Sigurd 1926 Osebergdronningens grav. In *Norge. Tidsskrift om vårt land. 2 årgang,* 21: 361–367.

Gräslund, Anne-Sofie 2001 The Position of Iron Age Scandinavian Women: Evidence from Graves and Rune Stones. In *Gender and the Archaeology of Death* edited by Bettina Arnold, and Nancy L. Wicker, pp. 81–104. Altamira Press, Walnut Creek.

Haugen, Hanne 2009 *Menn og deres perler: En studie av menns bruk av perler med hovedvekt på Midt-Norge i yngre jernalder.* Unpublished master dissertation, Universitetet iTrondheim, Trondheim.

Hays-Gilpin, Kelley, and David S. Whitley 1998 Introduction: Gendering the Past. In *Reader in Gender Archaeology,* edited by Hays–Gilpin, Kelley, and David S.Whitley, pp. 3–10. Routledge, London.

Hedeager, Lotte 1999 *Skygger av en annen virkelighet: Oldnordiske myter.* Pax Forlag, Oslo.

Hedeager, Lotte 2002 Åsgard rekonstruert. In *Mellom Himmel og Jord: Foredrag fra et seminar om religionsarkeologi* edited by Melheim, Lene, Lotte Hedeager, and Kristin Oma, pp156–183. Oslo Archaeological Series Vol. 2, Unipub, Oslo.

Heide, Eldar 2006 *Gand, seid og åndevind.* Avhandlig for graden docto artium (dr. Art). Universitetet i Bergen, Bergen.

Heyerdahl-Larsen, Birgit 1981 Gravfeltene i kaupangområdet. In *Kaupang-funnene. Bind 1* by Blindheim, Charlotte, Birgit Heyerdahl-Larsen, and Roar L. Tollnes, pp. 47–69. Universitetets Oldsaksamling, Oslo.

Heyerdahl-Larsen, Birgit 1995a Gravgjennomgang S. Bikjholberget/Lamøya. In *Kaupangfunnene, Bind II. Gravplassene Bikjholberget / Lamøya. Undersøkelsene 1950 – 57* by Blindheim, Charlotte, and Birgit Heyerdahl-Larsen, pp. 15–53. Universitetets Oldsaksamling, Oslo.

Heyerdahl-Larsen, Birgit 1995b Gravskikk. S. Bikjholberget/Lamøya. In *Kaupangfunnene, Bind II. Gravplassene Bikjholberget / Lamøya. Undersøkelsene 1950 – 57* by Blindheim, Charlotte, and Birgit Heyerdahl-Larsen, pp. 89–104. Universitetets Oldsaksamling, Oslo.

Hjørungdal, Tove 1991 *Det skjulte kjønn: patriarkal tradisjon og feministisk visjon i arkeologien belyst med fokus på en* jernalderkontekst. Acta archaeologica Lundensia. Series in no. 8, Vol. 19. University of Lund, Almqvist & Wiksell International, Lund.

Hodder, Ian 2001 Introduction: A Review of Contemporary Theoretical Debates in Arcaheology. In *Archaeological Theory Today* edited by Ian Hodder, pp. 1–13. Polity, Cambridge.

Hodder, Ian 2007 The 'Social' in archaeological Theory. In *A Companion to Social Archaeology*, edited by Meskell, Lynne, and Robert W. Preucel, pp. 23–42 Blackwell, Malden.

Hofseth, Ellen H. 1999 Historien bak handelskvinnene på Kaupang: kvinnegraver fra Vikingtid langs Vestfoldkysten. In *Viking. Norsk Arkeologisk Selskap:*101 – 128.

Hoftun, O. 1995 Jernaldersamfunnets Kvinnelighet. In *Kvinner i Arkeologi i Norge* 19–20: 94 –114.

Holck, Per 2009 *Skjelettene fra Gokstad og Osebergskipet.* Antropologiske skrifter nr. 8. Universitetet i Oslo, Oslo.

Hylland-Eriksen, Thomas 1995 *Small Places, Large Issues.* Pluto Press, London.

Høgestøl, Mari 1985 Endringer i Sosial Posisjon hos Jernalderens Kvinner. In *Kvinner i Arkeologi i Norge* 3:50–59.

Ingstad, Anne Stine 1982 The Functional Textiles from the Oseberg Ship. In *Textilsymposium Neumünster : archäologische Textilfunde.* Edited by Bender Jørgensen, Lise, and Klaus Tidow, pp. 85–96. Tekstilmuseum Neumynster, Nuemynster.

Ingstad, Anne Stine 1993a Tekstilene i Osebergskipet. In *Osebergdronningensgrav. Vår arkeologiske nasjonalskatt i nytt lys,* by Christensen, Arne Emil, Anne Stine Ingstad,

Bibliography

and Bjørn Myhre, pp. 176–208. Schibsted, Oslo.

Ingstad, Anne Stine 1993b Osebergdronningen. Hvem var hun? In *Osebergdronningensgrav. Vår arkeologiske nasjonalskatt i nytt lys,* by Christensen, Arne Emil, Anne Stine Ingstad, and Bjørn Myhre, pp. 224–258. Schibsted, Oslo.

Ingstad, Anne Stine 1995 The Interpretation of the Oseberg Find. In *The Ship as Symbol in Prehistoric and Medieval Scandinavia* edited by Christensen, Arne Emil, Anne Stine Ingstad, Ole Crumlin-Pedersen, and Birgitte Munch Thye, pp. 139–149. Publications from the National Museum, Studies in Archaeology and History Vol. 1, National Museum of Denmark department of Archaeology and Early History, Copenhagen.

Iversen, Frode 1999 Hva arvet Erlend? Om gods og godsproblematikk i yngre jernalder og middelalder. Et eksempel fra Etne i Hordaland. In *Et hus med mange rom: Vennebok til Bjørn Myhre på 60 års dagen. Bind B,* edited by Fuglestvedt, Ingrid, Terje Gansum, and Arnfrid Opedal, pp. 339–381. AmS Rapport Vol. 11, Stavanger Museum of Archaeology, Stavanger.

Jerpåsen, G. B. 2009 Application of Visual Archaeological Landscape Analysis: some Results. In *Norwegian Archaeology Review.* Vol. 42. No. 2. 2009: 123–144.

Jesch, Judith 1994 *Women in the Viking Age.* The Boydell Press, Woodbridge.

Jochens, Jenny 1995 *Women in Old Norse Society.* Cornell University Press, Ithaca, N.Y.

Jochens, Jenny 1996 *Old Norse Images of Women.* University of Pensylvania Press, Philadelphia.

Johansen, Lise-Marie Bye 2002 Perler i jernalder – kilde til mote i kvinnegraver og magi i mannsgraver. In *Mellom Himmel og Jord: Foredrag fra et seminar om religionsarkeologi* edited by Melheim, Lene, Lotte Hedeager, and Kristin Oma, pp 468–490. Oslo Archaeological Series Vol. 2, Unipub, Oslo.

Johnson, Matthew 1999 *Archaeological Theory: An Introduction.* Blackwell, Oxford.

Joyce, Rosemary A. 2007 Embodied Subjectivity: Gender, Feminity, Masculinity, Sexuality. In *A Companion to Social Archaeology ,* edited by Meskell, Lynne. and Robert W. Preucel, pp. 82–95. Blackwell, Malden.

Kearney, Amanda 2008 Living Landscapes: The Body and the Gender in Australian Landscape Archaeology. In *Handbook of Landscape Archaeology* edited by David, Bruno, and Julian Thomas, pp. 247–256. Left Coast Press, Walnut Creek.

Kobylinski, Zbigniew 1995 Ships, Society and Archaeologists. In *The Ship as Symbol in Prehistoric and Medieval Scandinavia* edited by Christensen, Arne Emil, Anne Stine Ingstad, Ole Crumlin-Pedersen and Birgitte Munch Thye, pp. 9–19. Publications from the National Museum, Studies in Archaeology and History Vol. 1, National Museum of Denmark department of Archaeology and Early History, Copenhagen.

Krafft, Sofie 1955 *Fra Osebergfunnets tekstiler: Fragmenter av Billedvever og silkestoffer med rekonstruerte monster.* Dreyer, Oslo.

Kristoffersen, Siv 1999a Swords and Brooches. Constructing Social Identity. In *Grave Matters. Eight studies of first milleium A burials in Crimea, England and Southern Scandinavia: papers from a session held at the European Association of Archaeologists Fourth Annual Meeting in Göteborg,* edited by Rundkvist, Martin, pp. 87–96. BAR International Series Vol. 781, BAR Publishing, Oxford .

Kristoffersen, Siv 1999b Symbolism and rites of transition in Iron Age Norway. In *Celebrations, Sanctuaries and the Vestiges of Cult activity. Papers from the Norwegian Institute in Athens, the 10th Anniversary Symposium of the Norwegian Institute at Athens, 12-16 May 1999,* edited by Wedde, Michael, pp. 287–303. Athens.

Kristoffersen, Siv 2000 *Sverd og Spenne. Dyreornamentikk og Sosial Kontekst.* Studia Humanitetis Bergensa, Høyskole Forlaget, Kristiansand.

Kristoffersen, Siv 2002 Selvbevisste vestlandsdamer i folkevandringstiden. In *Bondemotsand og sjølvkjensle på Sørvestlandet,* edited by Lindanger, Birger, pp. 3–12. Seminarrapport Ulstein Kloster, Haugaland Akademi.

Kristoffersen, Siv 2004a Bridal Jewels – In Life and Death. In *Combining the past and the present : archaeological perspectives on society : proceedings fromthe conference 'Pre-history in a global perspective' held inBergen, August 31st - September 2nd 2001, in honour of professor Randi Haaland's 60th anniversary,* edited by Oestigaard, Terje, Nils Anfinset, and Tore Saetesdal, pp. 31–37. BAR International series Vol. 1210, BAR Publishing, Oxford.

Kristoffersen, Siv 2004b Husfruen: Formiddling av fortidige roller. In *Feministisk teori, kvinne- og kjønnsforskning i Rogaland* edited by Selsing, Lotte, pp. 59–66. Stavanger: AmS – Varia Vol. 41. Stavanger Museum of Archaeology, Stavanger.

Kristoffersen, Siv, and Terje Oestigaard 2008 "Death Myths": Performing of Rituals and Variation in Corpse Treatment during the Migration Period in Norway. In *The Materiality of Death: Bodies, burials, beliefs,* edited by Fahlander, Fredrik, and Terje Oestigaard, pp. 127–139. BAR International Series Vol. 1768, Oxford

Lia, Øystein 2001 *Det Rituelle Rom. En fortolkende analyse av vikingtidens graver og landskap på*

Kaupang. Unpublished Masters dissertation, Universitetet i Oslo, Oslo.

Lia, Øystein 2002 Vikingtidens rituelle kompleksitet. In *Mellom Himmel og Jord: Foredrag fra et seminar om religionsarkeologi* edited by Melheim, Lene, Lotte Hedeager, and Kristin Oma, pp292–320. Oslo Archaeological Series Vol. 2, Unipub, Oslo.

Lillehammer, Grete 1989 Kvinnebønder i Nordens Forhistorie. In *Kvinner i Arkaeologi i Norge* 7:45–53.

Lillehammer, Grete 1996a *Død og Grav: Gravskikk på Kvassheim, Hå i Rogaland, SV Norge.* Ams Skrifter Vol. 13, Stavanger Museum of Archaeology, Stavanger.

Lillehammer, Grete 1996b Death, Family and Gender – Life's Starting Point. In *Kvinner i Arkeologi i Norge* 21:61 – 89.

Lucy, Sam 1997 Housewives, Warriors and Slaves? Sex and Gender in Anglo-Saxon Burials. In *Invisible People and Processes,* edited by Moore, Jenny, and Eleanor Scott, pp. 150–166. Leicester University Press, London.

Lund, Julie 2009 *Åsted og Vadested. Deponeringer, gjenstandbiografier og rumlig strukturering som kilde til vikingtidens kognitive landskaper.* Doktoravhandlinger forsvart ved det humanistiske fakultet, Universitetet i Oslo no. 389. Unipub, Oslo.

Lunde, Dagmar 1967 *Osebergdronningens billedteppe.* Universitetet i Oslo, Oslo.

Lundströmm, Inga, and Gundula Adolfsson 1995 *Den sterke kvinnen – fra Volve til Heks.* AmS-Småtrykk Vol. 27, Stavanger Museum of Archaeology, Stavanger.

Løken, P ia Skipper 2002 Rituelt Landskap - Gravfeltene på Store Dal og Hunn. In *Mellom Himmel og Jord: Foredrag fra et seminar om religionsarkeologi* edited by Melheim, Lene, Lotte Hedeager and Kristin Oma, pp 262–270. Oslo Archaeological Series Vol. 2, Unipub, Oslo.

Løken, Trond 1974 *Gravminner i Østfold og Vestfold. Et forsøk på en typologisk-kronologisk analyse og en religionshistorisk tolkning.* Dissertation for magister degree in Nordic Archaeology, Universitetet i Oslo, Oslo.

Myhre, Bjørn 1993a Ynglingeætten i Vestfold. In *Osebergdronningensgrav. Vår arkeologiske nasjonalskatt i nytt lys,* by Christensen, Arne Emil, Anne Stine Ingstad, and Bjørn Myhre, pp. 10–17. Schibsted, Oslo.

Myhre, Bjørn 1993b Arkeologiske kilder og ynglingeætten. In *Osebergdronningensgrav. Vår arkeologiske nasjonalskatt i nytt lys,* by Christensen, Arne Emil, Anne Stine Ingstad, and Bjørn Myhre, pp. 18–34. Schibsted, Oslo.

Myhre, Bjørn 1993c Diskusjon om ynglingeættens gravplasser. In *Osebergdronningensgrav. Vår arkeologiske nasjonalskatt i nytt lys,* by Christensen, Arne Emil, Anne Stine Ingstad, and Bjørn Myhre, pp. 35–50. Schibsted, Oslo.

Myhre, Bjørn 1994 Haugbrott eller gravplyndring i tidlig Kristen tid. In *Fra Hammer til Kors – 1000 år med Kristendom. Brytningstid i Viken,* edited by Hansen, Jan Ingar, and Knut G. Bjerva, pp. 68–85. Schibsted, Oslo.

Naumann, Elise 2006 *Identitet og samfunn på Kaupang. En fenomenologisk undersøkelse av gravenes metaforiske betydninger på Kaupang i Vestfold, yngre jernalder.* Unpublished Masters dissertation Universitetet i Oslo, Oslo

Näsman, Ulf 1994 Liv och död. Sydskandinaviska Grav och offerriter fran 200 till 1000 e. Kr.. In *Myte og Ritual i det Førkristne Norden: et symposium,* edited by Schjødt, Jens Peter, pp. 73–95. Odense Universitets Forlag, Odense.

Näsström, Britt-Mari 1994 Från Freyja til jungfru Maria vid religionsskiftet i Norden. In *Myte og Ritual i det Førkristne Norden: et symposium,* edited by Schjødt, Jens Peter, pp. 95–113. Odense Universitets Forlag, Odense.

Näsström, Britt-Mari 1995 *Freyja – the Great Goddess of the North.* Universitety of Lund, dep. of history of religions, Lund.

Næss, Jenny-Rita 1994 Kvinneliv i Sagatiden: En Statusrapport sett fra arkeologies ståsted og synspunkter på fremtidige forskningsoppgaver, in *Frøyas Hus: rapport fra fagseminaret "Kvinne- og dagligliv i sagatid", som ble holdt på Hamar 28.-29. april 1994,* edited by Foldøy, Oddveig, pp. 13 – 47. AmS Småtrykk Vol. 38, Stavanger Museum of Archaeology, Stavanger.

Omland, Atle 2002 Arkeologi, religion og folkelige forestillinger. In *Mellom Himmel og Jord: Foredrag fra et seminar om religionsarkeologi* edited by Melheim, Lene, Lotte Hedeager, and Kristin Oma, pp 32–51. Oslo Archaeological Series Vol. 2, Unipub, Oslo.

Opedal, Arnfrid 1998 *De glemte skipsgravene: Makt og myte på Avaldsnes.* AmS – Småtrykk Vol. 47, Stavanger Museum of Archaeology, Stavanger.

Pedersen, Unn 2000 *Vektlodd – sikre vitnesbyrd om handelsvirksomhet? Vektloddenes funksjoner i vikingtid. En analyse av vektloddmaterialet fra Kaupang og sørøst Norge.* Unpublished Masters dissertation. Universitetet i Oslo, Oslo.

Pedersen, Unn 2008 Dumme menn og troll til kjerringer. In *Facets of Archaeology; Essays in honour of Lotte Hedeager on her 60th birthday* edited by Childis, Konstantinos, Julie Lund, and Christopher Prescott, pp. 585–595. Oslo Arkeologiske Serie, Vol. 10, Unipub, Oslo.

Price, Neil 2002 *The Viking Way: Religion and War in Late Iron Age Scandinavia.* Dept. of Archaeology and Ancient History, Uppsala University, Uppsala.

Bibliography

Rainbird, Paul 2008 The Body and the Senses: Implications for Landscape Archaeology. In *Handbook of Landscape Archaeology* edited by David, Bruno, and Julian Thomas, pp. 263–271. Left Coast Press, Walnut Creek.

Ringstad, Bjørn 1987 De store gravminnene – et maktideologisk symbol? In *Viking, Norsk Arkeologisk selskap:* 65 – 77.

Rygh, Oluf 1999 [1985] *Norske Oldsager.* Tapir, Trondheim

Sass, Tina 1995 Translation of "the Funeral of the Rus-Chief" pages 87–92 of Ibn Fadlan. In *The Ship as Symbol in Prehistoric and Medieval Scandinavia* edited by Christensen, Arne Emil, Anne Stine Ingstad, Ole Crumlin-Pedersen, and Birgitte Munch Thye, pp. 136–138. Publications from the National Museum, Studies in Archaeology and History Vol. 1, National Museum of Denmark department of Archaeology and Early History, Copenhagen.

Schjødt, Jens Peter 1995 The Ship in Old Norse Mythology and Religion. In *The Ship as Symbol in Prehistoric and Medieval Scandinavia* edited by Christensen, Arne Emil, Anne Stine Ingstad, Ole Crumlin-Pedersen, and Birgitte Munch Thye, pp. 20–24. Publications from the National Museum, Studies in Archaeology and History Vol. 1, National Museum of Denmark department of Archaeology and Early History, Copenhagen

Sjøvold, Thorleif 1944 *Studier i Vestfolds Vikingtid.* Universitetets Oldsakssamling, Oslo.

Sjøvold, Thorleif 1971 *The Oseberg Find and the other Viking Ship finds.* Universitetets Oldsaksamling, Oslo.

Skogstrand, Lisbeth 2002 Religion + Kjønn = Gudinnearkeologi? En diskusjon mellom kjønn og religion som problemet i arkeologi med utgangspunkt i bronsealderen. In *Mellom Himmel og Jord: Foredrag fra et seminar om religionsarkeologi* edited by Melheim, Lene, Lotte Hedeager, and Kristin Oma, pp 450–467. Oslo Archaeological Series Vol. 2, Unipub, Oslo.

Skogstrand, Lisbeth 2006 Kjønn som analytisk kategori og kropslig kulturfenomen. In *Det Arkeologiske Kjønn* edited by Skogstrand, Lisbeth, and Ingrid Fuglestvedt, pp. 109–126. Oslo Arkeologiske Serie Vol. 7, Unipub, Oslo.

Skre, Dagfinn 1997 Hva betyr gravhaugene?. In *Middelalderens Symboler,* edited by Christensson, Ann, Else Mundal, and Ingvild Øye, pp. 37–49. Kulturtekster Vol. 11. Senter for Europeiske kulturstudier, Bergen.

Skre, Dagfinn 2007a Introduction". In *Kaupang in Skiringssal.,* edited by Skre, Dagfinn, pp. 13–24. Kaupang excavation project. Publication series Volume I. Norske Oldfunn 22 Vol 1. Aarhus University Press Kaupang Excavation Project, University of Oslo, Aarhus and Oslo.

Skre, Dagfinn 2007b The Skiringssal Cemetery. In *Kaupang in Skiringssal.,* edited by Skre, Dagfinn, pp. 363–384. Kaupang excavation project. Publication series Volume I. Norske Oldfunn 22 Vol 1. Aarhus University Press Kaupang Excavation Project, University of Oslo, Aarhus and Oslo.

Skre, Dagfinn 2007c Towns, Markets, Kings, Central Places. In *Kaupang in Skiringssal.,* edited by Skre, Dagfinn, pp. 445–469. Kaupang excavation project. Publication series Volume I. Norske Oldfunn 22 Vol 1. Aarhus University Press Kaupang Excavation Project, University of Oslo, Aarhus and Oslo.

Skre, Dagfinn and Frans-Arne Stylegar 2004 *Kaupang : vikingbyen : Kaupang-utstilling ved UKM 2004-2005.* University of Oslo, Oslo.

Solli, Brit 1999 Odin – the Queer? Om det skeive i norrøn mytologi. In *Et hus med mange rom: Vennebok til Bjørn Myhre på 60 års dagen. Bind B,* edited by Fuglestvedt, Ingrid, Terje Gansum, and Arnfrid Opedal, pp. 393–438. AmS Rapport Vol. 11, Stavanger Museum of Archaeology, Stavanger.

Stalsberg, Anne 2001 Visible Women made Invisble. Interpreting Varangian Women in Old Russia. In *Gender and the Archaeology of Death* edited by Bettina Arnold, and Nancy L. Wicker, pp. 65–80. Altamira Press, Walnut Creek.

Steinsland, Gro 1991 *Det hellige bryllup og norrøn kongeideologi.* Sollum, Oslo.

Steinsland, Gro 1994a Eros og død i norrøn kongeideologi: kan mytisk herskerideologi kaste lys over forestillinger og riter knyttet til død, begravelse og gravkult? In *Myte og Ritual i det Førkristne Norden: et symposium,* edited by Schjødt, Jens Peter, pp. 141–150. Odense Universitets Forlag, Odense .

Steinsland, Gro 1994b Fra Hedendom til Kristendom. In *Fra Hammer til Kors – 1000 år med Kristendom. Brytningstid i Viken,* edited by Hansen, Jan Ingar, and Knut G. Bjerva, pp. 17–31. Schibsted, Oslo.

Steinsland, Gro 2003 (ed). *Voluspå og andre norrøne helligtekster.* Den Norske Bokklubben, Oslo.

Strang, Veronica 2008 The Social Construction of Water. In *Handbook of Landscape Archaeology* edited by David, Bruno, and Julian Thomas, pp. 123–130. Left Coast Press, Walnut Creek.

Sturlason, Snorre 1943. *Snorres Kongesagaer.* Gyldedal Norsk Forlag, Oslo.

Stylegard, Frans-Arne 1995 *Dialoger med de døde: Arkeologien og gravskikken.* Unpublished Masters dissertation, Universitet i Oslo, Oslo.

Stylegar, Frans-Arne 1997 Gravskikk: Faghistoriske og teoretiske synspunkter. In *Konflikt i Forhistorien* edited by Fuglestvedt, Ingrid, and Bjørn Myhre, pp. 69–82. AmS-Varia Vol. 30, Stavanger Museum of Archaeology, Stavanger.

Stylegar, Frans-Arne 2007 The Kaupang Cemeteries Revisited. In *Kaupang in Skiringssal.,* edited by Skre, Dagfinn, pp. 65–126. Kaupang excavation project. Publication series Volume I. Norske Oldfunn 22 Vol. 1. Aarhus University Press Kaupang Excavation Project, University of Oslo, Aarhus and Oslo.

Svanberg, Fredrik 2003 *Death Rituals in South-East Scandinavia.* Almqvist og Wiksell International, Stockholm.

Synnestvedt, Anita 2006 Bildvävnaderna från Oseberg och haugen sett ur ett action/context for power perspektiv. In *Det Arkeologiske Kjønn* edited by Skogstrand, Lisbeth, and Ingrid Fuglestvedt, pp. 127–147. Oslo Arkeologiske Serie Vol. 7, Unipub, Oslo.

Thomas, Julian 2001 Archaeologies of Place and Landscape. In *Archaeological Theory Today* edited by Ian Hodder, pp. 165–186. Polity, Cambridge.

Tilley, Christopher 2008 Phenomenological Approaches to Landscape Archaeology. In *Handbook of Landscape Archaeology* edited by David, Bruno, and Julian Thomas, pp. 271–277. Left Coast Press, Walnut Creek.

Tollnes, Roar L. 1981 Den locale topografi og kommunikasjonsveien. In *Kaupang-funnene. Bind 1* Blindheim, Charlotte, Birgitte Heyerdahl-Larsen, and Roar L. Tollnes, pp.17–38. Universitetets Oldsaksamling, Oslo.

Tsigaridas, Z. 1998 Fra gård til grav: langhauger, kvinneroller og reproduksjon av samfunnet. In *Primitive Tider Arkeologisk Tidsskrift* 1998: 1–20.

Van Dyke, Ruth M 2008 Memory, Place and the Memorialization of Landscape. In *Handbook of Landscape Archaeology* edited by David, Bruno, and Julian Thomas, pp. 277–285. Left Coast Press, Walnut Creek.

Warmind, Morten 1995 Ibn Fadlan in the Context of his Age. In *The Ship as Symbol in Prehistoric and Medieval Scandinavia* edited by Christensen, Arne Emil, Anne Stine Ingstad, Ole Crumlin-Pedersen, and Birgitte Munch Thye, pp. 131–138. Publications from the National Museum, Studies in Archaeology and History Vol. 1, National Museum of Denmark department of Archaeology and Early History, Copenhagen.

Yilmaz, U. 2005 Kjønn og skjellett – menn og kvinner er ikke lenger det de engang var: En osteoarkeologisk undersøkelse av hvordan sosiale og biologiske faktorer påvirker uttrykket av skjelettets kjønn. In *Viking*:249 – 262.

Østmo, Mari 2002 Symbolikk i Landskapet – grenser, kosmologi og ritualer. In *Mellom Himmel og Jord: Foredrag fra et seminar om religionsarkeologi* edited by Melheim, Lene, Lotte Hedeager, and Kristin Oma, pp184–199. Oslo Archaeological Series Vol. 2, Unipub, Oslo.

www.ingramcontent.com/pod-product-compliance
Lightning Source LLC
Chambersburg PA
CBHW061549010526
44115CB00023B/2990